About
The *Holy*
Spirit

Mac Ward Symes

WESTBOW
PRESS®
A DIVISION OF THOMAS NELSON
& ZONDERVAN

WestBow Press books may be ordered through booksellers or by contacting:

You May Order From Publisher:
WestBow Press
A Division of Thomas Nelson & Zondervan
1663 Liberty Drive
Bloomington, IN 47403
www.westbowpress.com
844-714-3454

ISBN: 978-1-6642-2123-9 (sc)
ISBN: 978-1-6642-2124-6 (hc)
ISBN: 978-1-6642-2122-2 (e)

Library of Congress Control Number: 2021901299

Print information available on the last page.

WestBow Press rev. date: 09/08/2022

Contents

Contents

Preface

Holy Scripture contained in the Bible is the only source of truth that is authorized by God as the foundation of faith to be believed concerning him and his Kingdom.

- *2TI 3:16 All scripture is given by inspiration of God, and is profitable for doctrine, for reproof, for correction, for instruction in righteousness:*

The scripture gives detailed information regarding God himself, and regarding everything which God brought into existence through his miraculous creative ability. We learn that God begot a Son, and he empowered that Son to create all things that were created in earth and in heaven.

- *EPH 3:9 And to make all men see what is the fellowship of the mystery, which from the beginning of the world hath been hid in God, <u>who created all things by Jesus Christ</u>:*
- *HEB 1:2 Hath in these last days spoken unto us by his Son, whom he hath appointed heir of all things, <u>by whom also he made the worlds</u>;*

The scope of creation which God accomplished through his Son not only included the earth and its atmosphere, but also included heaven and all things therein.

- *COL 1:16 For <u>by him were all things created, that are in heaven</u>, and that are in earth, visible and invisible, whether they be thrones, or dominions, or principalities, or powers: all things were created by him, and for him:*
- *17 And he is before all things, and by him all things consist.*

As a part of all things which were created in heaven, and described as *"visible and invisible ... principalities, or powers,"* the Holy Spirit was doubtless brought into existence by God through his Son. There is no other Biblical explanation for the origination of the Holy Spirit.

The Holy Spirit became a dominant divine person who was in extremely close communion with God the Father and his Son. The three are designated in the Bible as *"The Godhead,"* and since creation they have worked together in close communication.

After the Son came to earth for a specific ministry, and then returned back to heaven so that he could work closely with his Father as the Head of the church, the Holy Ghost was sent to the church on earth to dwell within the bodies of every born again member of his church.

It is the author's desire to participate in the perfecting of the church that will doubtless occur in the last days. Today all doctrinal beliefs and practices of the church must come from the New Testament, with Christ, the apostles, and the early church as our foundation and pattern.

- *EPH 2: 20 And are built upon the foundation of the apostles and prophets, Jesus Christ himself being the chief corner stone;*

The New Testament is filled with information regarding the Holy Spirit. In fact a dominant message contained in the New

Testament regards the Holy Spirit, which is also called the Holy Ghost.

Most information regarding the Holy Ghost came from Jesus. God sent his only begotten Son to earth to give a plan of salvation whereby mankind could be forgiven for their sins, and obtain eternal life through God's grace.

God's plan was to first send his Son, who would accomplish his ministry on earth, and then the Son would return back to heaven to sit with his Father on his throne, to continue serving as the Head of the Church which he began before he left the earth. Paul prayed that the church would be strengthened by the Holy Spirit which was the "fullness of God" that would dwell in their inner man, which was the power that worked in them.

- *EPH 3:14 For this cause I bow my knees unto the Father of our Lord Jesus Christ,*

   15 Of whom the whole family in heaven and earth is named,

   16 That he would grant you, according to the riches of his glory, to be strengthened with might <u>by his Spirit</u> in the inner man;

   17 That Christ may dwell in your hearts by faith; that ye, being rooted and grounded in love,

   18 May be able to comprehend with all saints what is the breadth, and length, and depth, and height;

   19 And to know the love of Christ, which passeth knowledge, that ye might be filled with all the fulness of God.

   20 Now unto him that is able to do exceeding abundantly above all that we ask or think, according to the power that worketh in us,

   21 Unto him be glory in the church by Christ Jesus throughout all ages, world without end. Amen.

Besides sending his Son, a second phase of God's plan was to send the Holy Ghost to live within the bodies of every Christian member of that church because they believed in his Son Jesus Christ.

Jesus told his disciples that soon after his return to Heaven, the Holy Ghost would be sent to dwell within them. This was extremely important, expedient, and urgent to Jesus. The truth concerning the Holy Spirit is still extremely important today.

- *JOH 16:7 Nevertheless I tell you the truth; It is <u>expedient</u> for you that I go away: for if I go not away, the Comforter will not come unto you; but if I depart, I will send him unto you.*

Jesus knew the ministry of the Holy Ghost was vital to his church. He explained some important features of the ministry of the Holy Ghost.

- *JOH 16:8 And when he is come, he will reprove the world of sin, and of righteousness, and of judgment:*
  9 Of sin, because they believe not on me;
  10 Of righteousness, because I go to my Father, and ye see me no more;
  11 Of judgment, because the prince of this world is judged.
  12 I have yet many things to say unto you, but ye cannot bear them now.
  13 Howbeit when he, the Spirit of truth, is come, he will guide you into all truth: for he shall not speak of himself; but whatsoever he shall hear, that shall he speak: and he will shew you things to come.
  14 He shall glorify me: for he shall receive of mine, and shall shew it unto you.
  15 All things that the Father hath are mine: therefore said I, that he shall take of mine, and shall shew it unto you.

In the New Testament there is a treasure of information regarding the ministry of the Holy Spirit. Jesus said the following to his disciples.

- *ACT 1:8 But ye shall receive power, after that the Holy Ghost is come upon you: and ye shall be witnesses unto me both in Jerusalem, and in all Judaea, and in Samaria, and unto the uttermost part of the earth.*

The purpose of this book, according to its title, is to do an extensive Bible study "**ABOUT THE HOLY SPIRIT.**"

May God Bless,

Mac Ward Symes, Author

Introduction

This book is written for the benefit of anyone interested in the subject of the Holy Spirit. Throughout the world there is an increasing interest in the Holy Spirit, and about his ministry in the church, and also in the life of every Christian believer in which he dwells.

The names Holy Spirit and Holy Ghost are synonymous in meaning, and are both in the King James Version of the Bible, and are used interchangeably in the text of this book you are reading.

The purpose for this book is to make a thorough search of the Bible concerning subjects and questions "ABOUT THE HOLY SPIRIT."

The author has no interest in promoting any denominational doctrinal position. His sincere desire is to avoid doctrines and traditions of men, and to gain knowledge concerning the subject as recorded in the gospel of Christ.

There is a profound question in the Bible regarding the Holy Ghost:

- *1CO 6:19 What? know ye not that your body is the temple of the Holy Ghost which is in you, which ye have of God, and ye are not your own?*

20 For ye are bought with a price: therefore glorify God in your body, and in your spirit, which are God's.

Cordially and Prayerfully,
Mac Ward Symes
Author

1

Truth Unites

Christianity, as a faith has long been fragmented by many divisive factors which have splintered the body of Christian believers into a multitude of different theological camps. This book is not about division but is about unity among Christians. A deep commitment by the author to the unity of the body of Christ in the earth undergirds the writing of this book.

All Christians have for so long sung the rousing hymn, "Onward, Christian Soldiers." It is now time to march to the words of the song.

> *"Like a mighty army moves the church of God;*
> *Brothers, we are treading where the saints have trod;*
> *We are not divided; All one body we,*
> *One in hope and doctrine, One in charity."*

The Faith

- *JUD 1:3 Beloved, when I gave all diligence to write unto you of the common salvation, it was needful for me to write unto*

1

> *you, and exhort you that ye should earnestly contend for <u>the</u> <u>faith</u> which was once delivered unto the saints.*

"The faith" was once delivered to the saints. These saints comprised the early New Testament church in a pure form through the ministry of Christ. "The faith" was also delivered to the church through early apostles by whom a major portion of the New Testament was given to the church by the Holy Ghost. We are truly challenged to tread where saints have trod. The original revelation provides the only foundation on which the church must be built throughout succeeding generations.

- *EPH 2:20 And are built upon the foundation of the apostles and prophets, Jesus Christ himself being the chief corner stone;*
  21 In whom all the building fitly framed together groweth unto an holy temple in the Lord:
  22 In whom ye also are builded together for an habitation of God through the Spirit.

The things which happened to, and through, the early apostles are given as examples and patterns for the church to follow. They were filled with the Holy Spirit, and lived and walked in the Spirit, which means they were continually guided and taught by the Spirit. Their bodies became temples, or dwelling places, for the Holy Ghost, who lived within their spirit, mind, and body, exerting great control over their thoughts, actions, and emotions.

Jesus promised his disciples that when he returned back into heaven, he would ask the heavenly Father to send the Holy Ghost to dwell within his followers. I have selected a series of verses, all of them containing words spoken by Jesus during his last few days on earth. They show the emphasis (expedient urgency) Jesus placed on the Holy Spirit.

- *JOH 14:16 And I will pray the Father, and he shall give you another Comforter, that he may abide with you for ever;*
  17 Even the Spirit of truth; whom the world cannot receive, because it seeth him not, neither knoweth him: but ye know him; for he dwelleth with you, and shall be in you.
  26 ... But the Comforter, which is the Holy Ghost, whom the Father will send in my name, he shall teach you all things, and bring all things to your remembrance, whatsoever I have said unto you.
  27 ... Peace I leave with you, my peace I give unto you: not as the world giveth, give I unto you. Let not your heart be troubled, neither let it be afraid.
- *JOH 15:26 But when the Comforter is come, whom I will send unto you from the Father, even the Spirit of truth, which proceedeth from the Father, he shall testify of me:*
- *JOH 16:7 Nevertheless I tell you the truth; It is <u>expedient</u> for you that I go away: for if I go not away, the Comforter will not come unto you; but if I depart, I will send him unto you.*
  8 And when he is come, he will reprove the world of sin, and of righteousness, and of judgment:
  12 ... I have yet many things to say unto you, but ye cannot bear them now.
  13 Howbeit when he, the Spirit of truth, is come, he will guide you into all truth: for he shall not speak of himself; but whatsoever he shall hear, that shall he speak: and he will shew you things to come.
  14 He shall glorify me: for he shall receive of mine, and shall shew it unto you.
- *ACT 1:4 And, being assembled together with them, commanded them that they should not depart from Jerusalem, but wait for the promise of the Father, which, saith he, ye have heard of me.*

5 For John truly baptized with water; but ye shall be baptized with the Holy Ghost not many days hence.
8 ... But ye shall receive power, after that the Holy Ghost is come upon you: and ye shall be witnesses unto me both in Jerusalem, and in all Judaea, and in Samaria, and unto the uttermost part of the earth.

These verses provide a platform of Biblical support for the things contained in this book. To be more Biblically specific, they shall be the chief cornerstone support for the foundation of the apostles and prophets of the early New Testament church on which we are to build the church today.

Prior to the beginning of Christ's ministry John the Baptist, the forerunner of Christ, introduced Jesus as the one who would baptize believers in the Holy Ghost. This should indicate the importance of this truth, and alert all who believe in Christ, that they should be baptized in the Holy Ghost. John the Baptist said,

- *MAT 3:11 I indeed baptize you with water unto repentance: but he that cometh after me is mightier than I, whose shoes I am not worthy to bear: he shall baptize you with the Holy Ghost, and with fire:*

Since that original revelation concerning the Holy Ghost, carnal minds have veered from the truth, having substituted many doctrines and traditions of men in place of the gospel of the kingdom and the doctrines of Christ. During the centuries which followed the time of Christ and the early church, history reveals that men gradually replaced the truth with their religious traditions, as early as the third and fourth centuries, and an institutionalized church evolved, which gained control of the masses who embraced Christianity.

4

The church today is in a struggle to become un-entangled from doctrines which were derived ... not from Christ, neither from the apostles, nor the Bible ... but from traditions created by men. Only that which may be learned from Christ can be valid, and if any doctrine of the church today does not connect directly back to Christ and the apostles, it should not be tasted, handled or touched.

- *COL 2:21 (Touch not; taste not; handle not;*
  22 Which all are to perish with the using;) after the commandments and doctrines of men?
- *EPH 4:20 But ye have not so learned Christ; If so be that ye have heard him, and have been taught by him, as <u>the truth is in Jesus</u>:*

What a powerful statement --*"the truth is in Jesus."* Back to *the basics* should be the watchword of the church in these last days prior to the second coming of Christ. A constant preoccupation of the church should be to confirm truth which was once delivered to the saints (JUD 1:3).

Much of the truth which was delivered to the saints in the early church has been smothered by traditions of men.

- *MAR 7:13 Making the word of God of none effect through your tradition, which ye have delivered: and many such like things do ye.*

The truth will set believers free from the division and denominational fragmentation that has the church so fractured over the matter of the Holy Spirit. Christ, as the Prince of Peace is working on this problem with haste. The Holy Spirit is revealing truth to whomever he can find that will take what the word of God says over what their tradition says, or what they want to believe.

Before the turn of the twentieth century, hardly any emphasis had been placed upon the indwelling of the Holy Spirit. But in the mid eighteen-nineties, people began to claim experiences of being baptized in the Holy Ghost, just as it occurred on the day of Pentecost, complete with speaking in other tongues as the Spirit gave the utterance. Opposing doctrines began to crystallize. Since that time, a major doctrinal rift has divided the church over the issue of the baptism in the Holy Ghost and the manifestation of the gifts of the Spirit, especially speaking in other tongues (foreign languages).

For most, the Holy Spirit was like a new discovery since their churches and ministers had not given any information about him. The reality of the Holy Spirit became an exciting discovery which was enthusiastically and evangelistically shared by many. The new enthusiasts claimed that the infilling with the Holy Spirit was, according to the Bible, supposed to be accompanied by manifestations which had not been evident in the lives of Christians or in the church. In reply to this outbreak of what many people thought to be fanatical preoccupation with the Holy Ghost baptism, traditional theologians settled on the opinion that they had received the Holy Spirit when they were saved and had possessed him all along.

The new Holy Spirit movement rejected this claim that one receives the Holy Spirit at conversion. Their contention was that they had only been saved, but had not been baptized in the Holy Spirit because they had ignored, overlooked, or did not understand the truth about him. Furthermore, they took the position that speaking in tongues was the initial evidence of the indwelling of the Spirit, therefore, all who had not spoken in tongues had not received the Spirit.

The position of the latter was claimed to be the "full gospel," and new churches sprang up known as full gospel churches. The term "Pentecostal" became the identifier of the new movement. This name was derived from the day of Pentecost -- the day on which the Holy Ghost was first given to the church. The terms, *Pentecostal, full gospel, spirit filled,* and *holiness,* became terms and titles identifying the new movement. These were thorns in the side of the old-line traditionalists because it was as if Pentecostals were saying, "we are full gospel and you are not," or "we are spirit filled and you are not," etc.

Beginning in the nineteen-sixties, a secondary Pentecostal movement occurred. Those involved in this movement were mainly constituents of the old-line denominations. They identified themselves as *Charismatic,* and speaking in other tongues was given a new identifier ... *"glosalalia."* While they had become convinced regarding the Biblical authenticity of the baptism in the Holy Spirit -- complete with speaking in tongues, prophesying, the word of knowledge, the gift of healing, etc., -- The Charismatics did not particularly want to be associated with the old-line Pentecostals. This only enlarged the division which already existed among the family of God, because we now had a new branch of Pentecostals.

Many tried to hang onto their old denominational connections by terming themselves as *spirit-filled Baptists, spirit-filled Catholics, spirit-filled Methodist,* etc., right down the entire denominational line. Most were forced out of their denominational churches if they became too obvious or outspoken. Thousands of Charismatic churches sprang up all over the country and around the world. This movement had an impressive growth in a short period of time, and soon became a thorn in the side of traditionalism because of the emphasis on the operation of the gifts of the Spirit.

More emphasis was placed on prophesy and the "word of knowledge" than in the first Pentecostal movemet in the late nineteenth century and early twentieth century. In the Charismatic movement Strong emphasis was placed on speaking in tongues, while avoiding being identified as "Pentecostals."

Truth that can unite

The question facing the church today is, "what central, or basic truth could there possibly be that would unite brethren who are divided over man-made doctrinal issues?" Is it a hopeless cause? Are we too far gone?

I think not. The answer is in the word of God ... if one can find and accept it? It is the Holy Spirit's job to guide us into *"all truth."* He will not teach different things to different people! Can he guide us into this truth? A deeper question is, "do we want to be guided into truth that will unite us?" Or, are we afraid we might be forced to give up something having to do with our church ideas or doctrinal opinions?

Both sides must budge

The author comes from a strong traditional Pentecostal background, and yet, he has made adjustments to make provisions for what the word of God says, without any loss of truth, but rather gaining insight into essential truths. He believes God has revealed to him basic truth that can unite divided brethren -- Pentecostal and Non-Pentecostal.

It will be necessary for both sides of the issue to first listen, and then be willing to accept the word of God over tradition. All men will have to come to a better knowledge of truth. They will all be happier for having done so ... as they adhere to truth that is in the word of God.

The final authority

The first basic principle that must be established is, **the Bible is the word of God, and is the final authority on all matters of doctrinal truth.**

- *2TI 3:16 All scripture is given by inspiration of God, and is profitable for doctrine, for reproof, for correction, for instruction in righteousness:*
  17 That the man of God may be perfect, throughly furnished unto all good works.

The willingness to listen helps one to always be open for what *"thus sayeth the Lord."* All must believe that Christ intends to perfect his church, and to wash it with water by the word. This prevents one from closing their mind to revelation and the understanding of more truth.

- *EPH 5:26 That he might sanctify and cleanse it with the washing of water by the word,*
  27 That he might present it to himself a glorious church, not having spot, or wrinkle, or any such thing; but that it should be holy and without blemish.

Pentecostals and Non-Pentecostals have been so set in their ways doctrinally that there has been little room for dialogue or discussion. The time has come that both sides must discuss this issue openly and thoroughly. When there are two different doctrinal opinions, one has to be wrong ... and maybe both. At this point, let's say that both sides have been partially right. Hopefully, this book will be a timely contribution to the unity of the faith by helping both sides come to agreement concerning the one faith.

- *EPH 4:2 With all lowliness and meekness, with longsuffering, forbearing one another in love;*
  3 Endeavouring to keep the unity of the Spirit in the bond of peace.
  *4 There is one body, and **one Spirit**, even as ye are called in one hope of your calling;*
  *5 One Lord, <u>**one faith**</u>, one baptism,*
  6 One God and Father of all, who is above all, and through all, and in you all.

2

Opinions About Speaking in Other Tongues

Everyone must analyze the sources which have influenced their opinions concerning the baptism with the Holy Ghost and speaking in tongues, plus other gifts of the spirit, such as divine healing, or prophesy. One must determine if their opinions have been formed by others, rather than by the word of God. Opinions of friends, relatives, favorite ministers, and denominational doctrines can easily dominate what one believes.

Of course, there will be those who have never heard anything concerning the subject of the Holy Spirit, and it will all be new to them. Reading this book will open the subject in a constructive way.

Expedient

What the Bible has to say about the Holy Spirit is very clear and understandable, and yet there are divergent opinions about him and his ministry within the church … and within the individual believer. This is such vital information that Jesus used the word, *"expedient"* when speaking about the necessity for the Holy Ghost to be sent from heaven to dwell within the followers of Christ.

- *JOH 16:7 Nevertheless I tell you the truth; It is **expedient** for you that I go away: for if I go not away, the Comforter will not come unto you; but if I depart, I will send him unto you.*

Jesus knew he was about to return to be with his Father in heaven, and he planned to ask his Father to send the Holy Spirit to abide with the followers of Christ as a special comforter.

- *JOH 14:15 If ye love me, keep my commandments.*
  16 And I will pray the Father, and he shall give you another Comforter, that he may abide with you for ever;
  17 Even the Spirit of truth; whom the world cannot receive, because it seeth him not, neither knoweth him: but ye know him; for he dwelleth with you, and shall be in you.

Jesus considered this to be extremely urgent, meaning "expedient." The Holy Spirit receives truth from Christ and reveals it to those who believe in him. The Holy Spirit never teaches anything that does not agree with Christ and the Bible. The only way one can truly know and understand Christ is through the ministry of the Holy Spirit.

- *JOH 16:14 He shall glorify me: for he shall receive of mine, and shall shew it unto you.*

One's attention must be directed to the Holy Spirit in such a way that they will appreciate the extreme urgency (expediency) Christ placed upon the Holy Spirit's ministry. One must *receive* the Holy Spirit by faith in the same fullness, readiness, and open-mindedness that they receive Christ.

It is also necessary that *all* Christians receive the Biblical truth concerning the Holy Ghost with the same obedience that the disciples manifested when they remained in Jerusalem on the strength of Christ's promise that he would send them the Holy Spirit after he returned to heaven. Jesus explained very little about the Spirit, and even though they waited and tarried in prayer for ten days, they had little or no idea about what they were expecting to receive.

Speaking in a foreign language which was unknown to the speaker was doubtless a total surprise, and assumedly, God did it that way so they could have no preconceived input into the supernatural manifestation. Speaking in tongues was just as supernatural as the sound of a rushing mighty wind, and the appearance of cloven tongues of fire which sat upon each of them.

- *ACT 2:1 And when the day of Pentecost was fully come, they were all with one accord in one place.*
  2 And suddenly there came a sound from heaven as of a rushing mighty wind, and it filled all the house where they were sitting.
  3 And there appeared unto them cloven tongues like as of fire, and it sat upon each of them.
  4 And they were all filled with the Holy Ghost, and began to speak with other tongues, as the Spirit gave them utterance.

I am amazed at the unique ingenuity of God in his selection of tongues as a manifestation of the Spirit. There is no logical explanation for it. It completely surpasses human reasoning and intellect. It requires total faith in God's purposes and will. It requires total surrender of pride and ego. One must forego personal opinions and submit totally to God's will and plan. The opinions of others must hold no power nor generate fear. A commitment to

Christ as the baptizer requires total trust in his integrity, and also requires unswerving confidence in his word.

The last words spoken by Jesus just prior to his ascension were the following: *"these signs shall follow them that believe ... they shall speak with new tongues"* (MAR 16:17). These last words must have been extremely important to Jesus!

The refreshing

The disciples knew the Old Testament quite well, and only after the Holy Ghost had been given, did they fully understand ancient prophesies concerning the Spirit which had been given hundreds of years before.

- *ISA 28:11 For with stammering lips and another tongue will he speak to this people.*
  *12 To whom he said, This is the rest wherewith ye may cause the weary to rest; and **this is the refreshing**: yet they would not hear.*

Isaiah said prophetically *"this is the refreshing."* Peter made reference to this Old Testament passage almost immediately after the Holy Spirit was given on the day of Pentecost.

- *ACT 3:19 Repent ye therefore, and be converted, that your sins may be blotted out, when the **times of refreshing** shall come from the presence of the Lord.*
- *ACT 2:33 Therefore being by the right hand of God exalted, and having received of the Father the promise of the Holy Ghost, **he hath shed forth this, which ye now see and hear.***

The Great Teacher

It is not required that one understands the Holy Spirit before receiving him, because he is the teacher. One receives a teacher so they can be taught.

In the Tyndale House Book by Grace Livingston Hill entitled <u>Duskin</u>, (Soft Back Edition), we pick up the text on page 195 where Carol Berkley was reading her Bible seriously, which had not been her normal practice:

"She spent a good deal of the afternoon reading her Bible, and was amazed to find how interesting it had become. She knew nothing of the revealing power of the great Teacher the Holy Spirit, whom Christ promised should reveal the truth to the seeking heart."

Taken from (Title; *DUSKIN*) by Author: (Grace Livingston Hill). Copyright © (1929) by (J.B. Lippincott Company). Tyndale House Edition 1997. Used by permission of Tyndale House Publishers, Inc. All rights reserved.

It is the Holy Spirit who helps believers to understand God, Christ, and the gospel as revealed in the New Testament. Even Jesus knew his disciples would be unable to comprehend truth concerning the church and the ministry of the Holy Spirit prior to receiving the Spirit as an in-dwelling teacher, guide and comforter. Jesus said the following:

- *JOH 16:12 I have yet many things to say unto you, but ye cannot bear them now.*
  13 Howbeit when he, the Spirit of truth, is come, he will guide you into <u>all</u> truth: for he shall not speak of himself; but

whatsoever he shall hear, that shall he speak: and he will shew you things to come.

Many truths which Christ intended to impart to his church did not come directly in fullness through Christ personally. They were later revealed by the Holy Spirit through apostles who were chosen of God for this purpose. Jesus gave no detailed instructions concerning the structure of the church and how it was to function. He however made two important references to his church: that he was going to build his church: *"on this rock I will build my church"* (MAT 16:18), and that this church would have a framework of spiritual authority and organized social structure:

- *MAT 18:15 Moreover if thy brother shall trespass against thee, go and tell him his fault between thee and him alone: if he shall hear thee, thou hast gained thy brother.*
16 But if he will not hear thee, then take with thee one or two more, that in the mouth of two or three witnesses every word may be established.
17 And if he shall neglect to hear them, **tell it unto the church***: but if he neglect to hear the church, let him be unto thee as an heathen man and a publican.*
18 Verily I say unto you, Whatsoever ye shall bind on earth shall be bound in heaven: and whatsoever ye shall loose on earth shall be loosed in heaven.

The understanding of these things came after the Holy Ghost was given, and information came to, and through, the apostles as it was needed, and as the Holy Ghost led. Paul was caught up to the third heavens and he conversed directly with Christ who revealed to him the mystery concerning the church ... especially that it would consist of both Jews and Gentiles....

There is no way the disciples would have understood this prior to the death, resurrection, and ascension of Christ. It was only after the church began to function under the tutorship of the Holy Spirit that answers could be understood as they were needed. Jesus said the Holy Ghost would show them things to come:

- *JOH 16:13 Howbeit when he, the Spirit of truth, is come, he will guide you into all truth: for he shall not speak of himself; but whatsoever he shall hear, that shall he speak: and **he will shew you things to come.***

While the apostle Paul was clearly given the ministry as the foundation builder for the church, he shared these truths with the other apostles, and they discerned the will of God through the guidance of the Holy Spirit. As a result, today we have the portion of the New Testament which follows the four gospels ... which was given to men by the Holy Spirit ... and which contains the guidelines for the church to be accepted as being the established will of God.

This takes nothing away from Christ as the head of the church, but adds to the relationship as we see his promise to the apostles fulfilled. This is why Paul gave a picture of the church as a structure built upon Christ as the only foundation.

- *1CO 3:10 According to the grace of God which is given unto me, as a wise masterbuilder, I have laid the foundation, and another buildeth thereon. But let every man take heed how he buildeth thereupon.*
11 For other foundation can no man lay than that is laid, which is Jesus Christ.

And yet, Paul understood fully the part the apostles were playing in the laying of this foundation. It was systematically developed by the Holy Spirit through the ministry of the apostles and prophets of the New Testament church. In another distinctly separate and different analogy Paul depicted the foundation as consisting of the apostles and prophets with Christ being the chief corner stone.

- *EPH 2:20 And are built upon the foundation of the apostles and prophets, Jesus Christ himself being the chief corner stone;*
  21 In whom all the building fitly framed together groweth unto an holy temple in the Lord:
  22 In whom ye also are builded together for an habitation of God <u>through the Spirit</u>.

The last phrase of the above passage says, *"through the Spirit."* This is one of many scriptures which confirms the Holy Spirit's involvement in the development and understanding of truth which Christ revealed after he had returned to his throne in heaven.

The Holy Spirit wrote the book

The reason that the Holy Spirit is designated as the Teacher of Biblical truth is because he wrote the book.

- *2PE 1:20 Knowing this first, that no prophecy of the scripture is of any private interpretation.*
  21 For the prophecy came not in old time by the will of man: ***but holy men of God spake as they were moved by the Holy Ghost.***

The Holy Ghost moved upon those who wrote the book. This is why the Holy Ghost is designated as the divine teacher. My brother, Rodney Symes, was a student at the University of Illinois.

He said that many of their textbooks had been written by the professor teaching the class. Rodney said, "If you want a great teacher, study under the professor who wrote the book."

This is why it is so important today for believers to be walking in the fullness of the Spirit. This means walking in all the ways the Spirit manifests himself to and through believers. A main emphasis of this book you are reading has to do with speaking in other tongues and its significance and importance. An all-out effort is put forth to explain Biblically why one should ... speak in tongues. But, there are many other aspects of the indwelling of the Holy Spirit besides speaking in tongues. The first, and simplest reason to believe is, because Jesus said the following as his last words before his ascension back to heaven.

- *MAR 16:17 And these signs shall follow them that believe; In my name shall they cast out devils; <u>they shall speak with new tongues;</u>*

Speaking in new tongues was listed among several supernatural spiritual signs that shall " *follow*," or accompany "*them that believe*." This applies to all believers. If there are any intrinsic benefits in speaking in tongues, then Jesus meant them for the good of *all* Christians. There must be some beneficial reason that Paul spoke in tongues.

- *1CO 14:18 I thank my God, I speak with tongues more than ye all:*

When one speaks in tongues they are speaking to God. While the one speaking does not understand what is being said, the Spirit is, nonetheless communicating with God through them ... making intercession for them <u>according to the will of God.</u> In later chapters we will research this in great detail, but at this point let it suffice to say that, if Christ thought it *"expedient"* that the Holy Ghost should come, then all believers must hold the matter as significantly important.

- *ACT 10:45 And they of the circumcision which believed were astonished, as many as came with Peter, because that on the Gentiles also was poured out the gift of the **Holy** Ghost. 46 **For they heard them speak with tongues**, and magnify God.*

Speaking in tongues is a scriptural sign that the Holy Spirit has taken up his abode within a believer's body.

- *1CO 14:22 Wherefore tongues are for a sign.*
- *1CO 6:19 What? know ye not that your body is the temple of the Holy Ghost which is in you, which ye have of God …*

As the Spirit gave them utterance

No one should down-play, deny, or reject speaking in other tongues ...as the Spirit gives the utterance. If speaking in tongues comes from any other source, even from the speakers own mind, then it is not by the Spirit.

- *ACT 2:4 And they were all filled with the Holy Ghost, and began to speak with other tongues **as the Spirit gave them utterance**.*

The Holy Spirit was extremely important to Jesus because he knew that after he returned to be with his Father in Heaven, the Father would send the Holy Ghost to earth to dwell within everyone who was saved through faith in Jesus.

Jesus said it was expedient, meaning extremely urgent that

he go back to heaven, so that the Holy Ghost would come to the church to dwell within the bodies of the saints, who would serve as his witnesses throughout the world. Jesus made some important statements concerning the Holy Ghost.

- *JOH 16:7 Nevertheless I tell you the truth; It is expedient for you that I go away: for if I go not away, the Comforter will not come unto you; but if I depart, I will send him unto you.*
- *ACT 1:8 But ye shall receive power, after that the Holy Ghost is come upon you: and ye shall be witnesses unto me both in Jerusalem, and in all Judaea, and in Samaria, and unto the uttermost part of the earth.*
- *MAR 16:17 And these signs shall follow them that believe; In my name shall they cast out devils; they shall speak with new tongues;*

Speaking with new tongues is also called speaking in **other** tongues, such as occurred on the day of Pentecost when the Holy Ghost came to dwell within Christians as Jesus had predicted.

- *ACT 2:4 And they were all filled with the Holy Ghost, and began to speak with **other tongues**, as the Spirit gave them utterance.*

Speaking in other tongues is a miracle because one is speaking in a language which is totally foreign to them, but is a valid language that is known and used somewhere in the world. This miracle has been confirmed many times, and records are given in this book you are reading where persons familiar with a foreign language understood what was being spoken in other tongues by the Holy Ghost. (Chapter 10)

Interpretation of tongues

When a congregation of Christians meet together such as in church, normally they all speak the same language, and if someone speaks in tongues by the Spirit, no one can understand that which is spoken. The Bible covers this situation with instructions concerning a gift of the Spirit which is called the **gift of interpretation of tongues**. The following passage gives a list of nine gifts of the Spirit which are ways these gifts are manifested to the church by the Holy Spirit. **Interpretation of tongues is included in this list.**

- *1CO 12:7 But the manifestation of the Spirit is given to every man to profit withal.*
  8 For to one is given by the Spirit the word of wisdom; to another the word of knowledge by the same Spirit;
  9 To another faith by the same Spirit; to another the gifts of healing by the same Spirit;
  *10 To another the working of miracles; to another prophecy; to another discerning of spirits; to another divers kinds of tongues; to another **the interpretation of tongues:***
  11 But all these worketh that one and the selfsame Spirit, dividing to every man severally as he will.

The gift of **interpretation** of tongues is a miracle which may occur after someone has spoken in tongues while the congregation listens, but does not understand the language being spoken. Then another person speaking supernaturally by the Holy Ghost interprets in the language of the congregation that which was spoken in tongues. Scriptural information concerning this is the following:

- *1CO 14:26 How is it then, brethren? when ye come together, every one of you hath a psalm, hath a doctrine, hath a tongue, hath a revelation, __hath an interpretation__. Let all things be done unto edifying.*
  27 If any man speak in an unknown tongue, let it be by two, or at the most by three, and that by course; and let one __interpret__.
  28 But if there be no interpreter, let him keep silence in the church; and let him speak to himself, and to God.
  29 Let the prophets speak two or three, and let the other judge.

Why is speaking in other tongues important? It is important because when the Holy Spirit speaks through a person in other tongues, they are not speaking to men, but they are **speaking to God**, which is extremely important.

- *1CO 14:2 For he that speaketh in an unknown tongue speaketh not unto men, __but unto God__: for no man understandeth him; howbeit in the spirit he speaketh mysteries.*

Wonderful works of God

Another important aspect concerning speaking in tongues is that one may be worshipping and praising God, and magnifying him for his many wonderful works, such as happened on the day of Pentecost.

- *ACT 2:7 And they were all amazed and marvelled, saying one to another, Behold, are not all these which speak Galilaeans?*
  8 And how hear we every man in our own tongue, wherein we were born?

9 Parthians, and Medes, and Elamites, and the dwellers in Mesopotamia, and in Judaea, and Cappadocia, in Pontus, and Asia,
10 Phrygia, and Pamphylia, in Egypt, and in the parts of Libya about Cyrene, and strangers of Rome, Jews and proselytes,
11 Cretes and Arabians, **we do hear them speak in our tongues the wonderful works of God.**

Intercession for us

Another important ministry of the Holy Spirit is **Intercession**. The Holy Spirit communicates with God on our behalf. Therefore, when one prays or speaks in other tongues the Holy Spirit is either worshipping and magnifying God, or he is interceding with God concerning important spiritual and physical needs, on behalf of the person through whom he is speaking. He may be also praying concerning the needs of others with whom we are associated, such as loved ones.

- *ROM 8:26 Likewise the Spirit also helpeth our infirmities: for we know not what we should pray for as we ought: but the Spirit itself maketh **intercession** for us with groanings which cannot be uttered* (which we could not utter).

It is God who searches our hearts because he loves us and is aware of everything pertaining to our lives. He knows what is on the mind of the Spirit when he makes intercession for us, and the Spirit always asks *"according to the will of God."*

- *ROM 8:27 And he that searcheth the hearts knoweth what is the mind of the Spirit, because he maketh intercession for the saints according to the will of God.*

All speaking in tongues is important, whether it be worship and praise or intercession, because it is all speaking with God. The apostle Paul believed in speaking in tongues.

- *1CO 14:18 I thank my God,* ***I speak with tongues more than ye all:***

- *1CO 14:5* ***I would that ye all spake with tongues*** *but rather that ye prophesied: for greater is he that prophesieth than he that speaketh with tongues, except he interpret, that the church may receive edifying.*

Whether speaking in other tongues, or speaking prophetically in the native language of the people … all is spoken by the anointing of the Holy Ghost!

It is incumbent upon ministers of Christ today to keep this truth alive and in the forefront of doctrinal values. One should hunger for the full manifestation of speaking in other tongues as a sign which gives evidence of the infilling of the Holy Spirit. Jesus said,

- *MAT 5:6 Blessed are they which do hunger and thirst after righteousness: for they shall be filled.*

The nearer we get to the second coming of Christ, and to the intense world conditions politically, socially, economically, and spiritually that are prophetically predicted to be associated with that time, the need for the baptism in the Holy Ghost intensifies greatly.

The great last day outpouring if the Spirit

The day of Pentecost was a great outpouring that continues today, but the greatest outpouring (prophesied by Joel) is yet to come, and will occur shortly before the second coming of Christ. It is called The Great Tribulation, which is a seven-year period of very intense persecution of saints by the Antichrist, which will bring about a world-wide harvest of souls and a mass uniting of Christianity as the body of Christ.

Peter was able to quote from Joel, who had prophesied concerning a great outpouring of the Holy Spirit which would take place in the last days. The day of Pentecost was not the complete fulfillment of Joel's prophesy because it did not take place during the end time which Peter called *"the last days"* which immediately precedes the day when the Lord comes to earth again:

- *ACT 2:17 And it shall come to pass in <u>the last days</u>, saith God, I will pour out of my Spirit upon all flesh: and your sons and your daughters shall prophesy, and your young men shall see visions, and your old men shall dream dreams:*

  18 And on my servants and on my handmaidens I will pour out in those days of my Spirit; and they shall prophesy:

  19 And I will shew wonders in heaven above, and signs in the earth beneath; blood, and fire, and vapour of smoke:

  20 The sun shall be turned into darkness, and the moon into blood, before the great and notable <u>day of the Lord come:</u>

Time or space will not permit me to go into an extensive study concerning Joel's prophesy regarding the last days. But, I will say, the Prophet Joel warned concerning a time which would come just prior to the second coming of Christ, when the entire world would be devastated by terrible distress and calamities. Joel must have been seeing the great last-days tribulation that is also prophesied in other Biblical scriptural locations.

In fact, every person on earth will be so distressed with the hopeless, impossible world conditions globally, financially, politically, with drought, starvation, evil wars, riots, raging death, ravaging Satanic forces ... so impossible that mankind in general will see that God holds the only possible help or solution.

The Book of Joel contains prophetic insight which had been revealed to Joel by the Holy Spirit. He was given special revelations concerning events that would occur in the time period surrounding the earthly ministry of Christ.

"The vision of the wonder-working Spirit leads right up to the events that precedes and ushers in the advent of Christ. Chapter 2 contains the picture and prophecy of His coming. It is full of profound prophetic interest.

"Among its pictures are the restoration of Israel from their long captivity, the final conflict of ungodly nations against Christ and His people, the great battle of Armageddon, the second coming of the Lord Jesus Christ, and the establishment of His blessed kingdom."

From reading the Book of Joel we learn that it is during this time that Israel, as a nation will turn to God, and repent for crucifying Jesus (ZEC 12:10). There will be such an enormous spiritual revival that much of the world's population, along with Israel, will turn to God in repentance.

It is during these last-days that Joel sees a great outpouring of the Spirit on every repentant sinner, so much that the Bible says God will pour out the Holy Spirit on "all flesh."

- *ACT 2:17 And it shall come to pass in the last days, saith God, I will pour out of my Spirit upon all flesh.*

The above verse is quoted from Joel 2:28. Peter knew the outpouring of the Holy Spirit on the day of Pentecost was the same Holy Spirit which God would pour out in the last days.

- *JOE 2:28 And it shall come to pass afterward, that <u>I will pour out my spirit upon all flesh</u>; and your sons and your daughters shall prophesy, your old men shall dream dreams, your young men shall see visions:*
  29 And also upon the servants and upon the handmaids in those days will I pour out my spirit.

In Acts 2:33, Peter said the Spirit in Joel 2:28 was the same Holy Ghost that right then was being poured out on the day of Pentecost.

- *ACT 2:33 Therefore being by the right hand of God exalted, and having received of the Father the promise of the **<u>Holy Ghost</u>**, he hath shed forth this, which ye now see and hear.*

At this present time one would be foolish to ignore the reality or importance of the Holy Ghost in their current life. Many Christians today, who seem to have little interest in the Holy Ghost and the gifts of the Spirit, will at that time welcome the spiritual power and help of the Holy Ghost. When they are so distressed because of world conditions spiritually and politically, and they do not know what or how to pray, they will welcome the intercession of the Holy Spirit as he prays in other tongues for them and their needs.

- *ROM 8:26 Likewise the Spirit also helpeth our infirmities: for we know not what we should pray for as we ought: but the Spirit itself maketh intercession for us with groanings which cannot be uttered (which we could not utter).*
- *27 And he that searcheth the hearts knoweth what is the mind of the Spirit because he maketh intercession for the saints according to the will of God.*

Why wait until distressing times come? Everyone needs the help and comfort of the Holy Spirit daily. Doesn't it seem reasonable that one should be learning about the fullness of the experience right now, rather than wait?

It is to this assumption that the author directs this book because he believes he has already experienced many marvelous events in his life that have resulted from the working of the Holy Ghost. Also, the manifestation of the gift of speaking in other tongues has been confirmed as a truly miraculous operation of the Spirit that has incalculable benefits to the believer. This will all come out as these matters are woven into the fabric of the text in this book.

3

Administrations, Operations, Manifestations

GIFTS OF THE SPIRIT

At this point I want to call attention to the **gifts** of the Spirit. When a person receives the gift of the Holy Ghost, there is more. First Corinthians, Chapter twelve, Verses 8 through 10, tells us the Holy Ghost brings with him nine (9) supernatural gifts that are available to spirit-filled believers. Verses 5 and 6 in the same passage inform us that these gifts are given by the Lord (Jesus) and by God, and are administered and operated, and "worketh" through the ministry of the Holy Spirit (V. 11).

I recently heard a famous Television Minister preach on the Subject of the Holy Spirit, and during a detailed message concerning the Person and Godhead of the Holy Spirit, he covered practically every important Biblical aspect of the Holy Spirit, but he ignored one of the most prominent features of the ministry of the Holy Spirit. That discarded feature reflected his denominational persuasion, and had to do with the **gifts** of the Holy Spirit, which

Biblically gives the most dominant purpose for which the Holy Ghost was given to the church.

The purpose of the Holy Spirit is to empower the church to manifest God's power through supernatural gifts of the Holy Ghost. After Christ ascended back to Heaven, the disciples went preaching everywhere, and the Lord worked with them by confirming the word with **signs**, meaning manifestations of the gifts of the Spirit.

- *MAR 16:19 So then after the Lord had spoken unto them, he was received up into heaven, and sat on the right hand of God. 20 And they went forth, and preached everywhere, the Lord working with them, and confirming the word with signs following.*

One must not underestimate the importance of the **gifts** of the Holy Ghost.

- *1CO 12:1 Now concerning spiritual gifts, brethren, I would not have you ignorant.*
  4 Now there are diversities of gifts, but the same Spirit.
  5 And there are differences of administrations, but the same Lord.
  6 And there are diversities of operations, but it is the same God which worketh all in all.
  7 But the manifestation of the Spirit is given to every man to profit withal.
  *8 For to one is given by the Spirit the **word of wisdom**; to another the **word of knowledge** by the same Spirit;*
  *9 To another **faith** by the same Spirit; to another the **gifts of healing** by the same Spirit;*

*10 To another the **working of miracles**; to another **prophecy**; to another **discerning of spirits**; to another **divers kinds of tongues**; to another the **interpretation of tongues**:*
*11 But **all these worketh that one and the selfsame Spirit**, dividing to every man severally as he will.*

Concerning the gift of speaking in other tongues which is being emphasized in this book you are reading, I will point out in verse ten (10) that "**tongues**" is included within this list of spiritual gifts. In fact, it is a dominant topic in the Gospel of Christ through the New Testament.

In other scriptural passages "tongues" is also called "languages," and "voices." When the gift of the Holy Ghost was given on the day of Pentecost, when disciples were speaking in other tongues, they were speaking in the foreign languages of fifteen different nations. In verse ten (10) above it says "diverse kinds of tongues." "Diverse" means "different or various" kinds of languages.

The Holy Spirit has access to thousands of known languages. An internet Google search reveals the following:

How many languages are there in the world? | Ethnologue
https://www.ethnologue.com › guides › how-many-lan...

7,139 **languages** are spoken today,

In the New Testament there are numerous passages pertaining to the Holy Spirit regarding speaking in other tongues. They all cannot be included in the text of this book, but a few are here given for your personal study.

Romans 12:5-10
1 Corinthians 12:27-31
1 Corinthians 14:1-6

1 Corinthians 14:8-19
1 Corinthians 14:23-25
1 Corinthians 14:26-32
Ephesians 4:8
Ephesians 6:18

A sincere believer in Christ must take serious care concerning the subject of the Holy Ghost, and the gift of speaking in other tongues, because the Bible says so much about the subject. It is certainly an important subject of interest to Christ and to God his Father.

- *HEB 2:3 How shall we escape, if we neglect so great salvation; which at the first began to be **spoken by the Lord**, and was confirmed unto us by them that heard him;*

Jesus was the first person to mention "tongues" in the New Testament. Also, God willingly participated in the ministry of the Holy Spirit.

*4 **God also bearing them witness**, both with signs and wonders, and with divers miracles, and **gifts of the Holy Ghost**, according to his own will? ... (and speaking in tongues was one of those **gifts**.)*

Jesus spoke the following which confirms that he and his heavenly Father both believed in the **gifts** of the Holy Spirit.

- *LUK 11:13 If ye then, being evil, know how to give good **gifts** unto your children: **how much more shall your heavenly Father give the Holy Spirit to them that ask him?***

Jesus endorsed the gift of speaking in other languages by the utterance of the Holy Ghost.

- *MAR 16:17 And these signs shall follow them that believe; In my name shall they cast out devils; they shall speak with new tongues;*

Scripturally there are *"diversities of gifts,"* or different kinds of gifts, but they all come from the same, one-and-only Holy Spirit. These manifestations are found in First Corinthians, Chapter twelve, and are referred to as *"administrations," "operations,"* and *"manifestations of the Spirit."* These three words are found in the following passage.

- *1CO 12:4 Now there are diversities of gifts, but the same Spirit.*
  *5 And there are differences of **administrations**, but the same Lord.*
  *6 And there are diversities of **operations**, but it is the same God which worketh all in all.*
  *7 But the **manifestation** of the Spirit is given to every man to profit withal.*

These are ways the Holy Spirit works through individual Christians as members of the body of Christ ... He administers, He operates, He manifests.

It is incumbent upon all believers to accept all the *"administrations," "operations,"* and *"manifestations,"* as being in full force and operational in the church today including the gift of healing, working of miracles, prophesy, speaking in tongues, the interpretation of tongues, plus the rest.

- *1CO 12:11 But all these worketh that one and the selfsame Spirit, dividing to every man severally as he will.*

12 For as the body is one, and hath many members, and all the members of that one body, being many, are one body: so also is Christ.

Verse 12 is extremely important because it places the functioning of all the gifts within the body of Christ which is the church. This Verse is also important because it involves every single member of the body. Included is every person who has been saved by the grace of God. Scripturally, this means they are a responsible member of the body of Christ, which is the church.

Chapter 12 is summarized by the following Verses.

- *1CO 12:27 Now ye are the body of Christ, and members in particular.*
  28 And God hath set some in the church, first apostles, secondarily prophets, thirdly teachers, after that miracles, then gifts of healings, helps, governments, <u>diversities of tongues</u>.

A cardinal Biblical truth is that God, himself set the gift of tongues in the church, along with all other gifts. Yes, every member must believe and receive this truth, and none is exempted, therefore every person who has been placed into Christ should embrace the truth regarding all gifts of the Spirit. This answers the question, *"should all speak with tongues?,"* with a resounding "YES."

This outlines God's plan concerning the place of the Holy Spirit and his gifts within the body of Christ. The church is not a denomination, nor a combination of denominations. The church consists of every person on the face of the earth who has been placed into Christ ... Jew or Gentile, male or female, bond or free.

- *1CO 12:13 For by one Spirit are we all baptized into one body, whether we be Jews or Gentiles, whether we be bond or free; and have been all made to drink into one Spirit.*

Non-Pentecostals

Denominations and individuals, who consider themselves as Non-Pentecostals, usually accept or practice some, but not all, of the above gifts of the Spirit. Their favorite gifts are wisdom, knowledge, and prophesying, with prophesying equated to preaching. Endowments of wisdom and knowledge, whether natural or acquired through educational processes, meet their qualifications for the gifts of wisdom and knowledge. For them, applying this wisdom and knowledge through preaching, teaching, or public speaking, is equated to prophesying ... with little emphasis on supernatural Holy Spirit endowments involved.

All true gifts of the Spirit are manifestations of the Spirit, and are not displays of human intelligence or ability. Emphasis must be placed on their *supernatural* qualities. In this book *speaking in tongues* serves as a focal point which is illustrative and connected with all the other gifts. A sincere attempt is being made to <u>rightly divide</u> the word of truth so clearly and accurately that anyone can see precisely what the Bible says about truth regarding the Holy Spirit and his gifts.

- *2TI 2:15 Study to shew thyself approved unto God, a workman that needeth not to be ashamed, rightly dividing the word of truth.*

Love is the glue

Christian love for Christ can be demonstrated only to, and through, those around us. Jesus said, *"when you do it* (show love and kindness) *to the least of my disciples, ye do it unto me."* We are told that *"charity is the bond of perfectness"* (COL 3:14) -- thus, is the glue (*"bond"*) that binds the Children of God in fellowship around Christ.

The spiritual force behind this unity is the Holy Spirit. Christians have been called to the **vocation** of functioning in life as a member of the body of Christ. One must walk in a way-of-life that befits this lifestyle ... worthy of participating in the united fellowship of the saints. A conscious effort must be made by all disciples of Christ to endeavor, or put forth, whatever effort it takes to see that the bond of love is not broken, nor the fellowship divided and fragmented by doctrines of men, or for any other reason.

- *EPH 4:1 I therefore, the prisoner of the Lord, beseech you that ye walk worthy of **the vocation** wherewith ye are called,*
  2 With all lowliness and meekness, with longsuffering, forbearing one another in love;
  3 Endeavouring to keep the unity of the Spirit in the bond of peace.
  4 There is one body, and one Spirit, even as ye are called in one hope of your calling;

God's last day gift

Warning is given in New Testament Scripture concerning perilous times that shall come in the last days. A lack of love characterizes the normal human relationships. We are warned that men will be lovers of their own selves.

- *2TI 3:1 This know also, that in the last days perilous times shall come.*
  2 For men shall be lovers of their own selves ...

Love is a fruit of the Holy Spirit

- *GAL 5:22 **But the fruit of the Spirit is love**, joy, peace, longsuffering, gentleness, goodness, faith,*
  23 Meekness, temperance: against such there is no law.

Members within the church, as the body of Christ, are instructed to forbear with one another in love. As an answer to the pressures of *"the last days,"* God gives the Holy Spirit to every believer. It is imperative that this spiritual love relationship be active in the church, and not dormant, alive and not dead, positive and not negative, real and not a pretense.

The indwelling of the Holy Spirit gives the power to manifest spiritual love as a fruit of the Spirit. This magnifies the serious need for the indwelling of the Holy Spirit as God's divine source of love.

The gospel of the kingdom

When Jesus gave his dissertation concerning the end-times, He concluded with this statement:

- *MAT 24:14 And **this gospel of the kingdom** shall be preached in all the world for a witness unto all nations; and then shall the end come.*

> *MAR 16:15 And he said unto them, Go ye into all the world, and preach the gospel to every creature.*
> *MAR 16:17 And these signs shall follow them that believe; In my name shall they cast out devils; they shall speak with new tongues;*

Consider the phrase, *"this gospel of the kingdom."* This means the truth ... the gospel truth ... shall be preached throughout the world. One should have no greater aspiration than to be a preacher of the gospel truth. The gospel is the truth as Jesus knows it ... the gospel of Christ.

The gospel of the kingdom is the truth about the objectives of Christ concerning his kingdom ... both now and in the future -- that of ruling his kingdom from the vantage point of his Father's throne in heaven. This unseen kingdom does not come at the present time *"with observation"* (visibly), but is within the believers.

- *LUK 17:20 And when he was demanded of the Pharisees, when the kingdom of God should come, he answered them and said, The kingdom of God cometh not with observation: 21 Neither shall they say, Lo here! or, lo there! for, behold, the kingdom of God is within you.*

The Kingdom of Christ will come literally and visibly when Jesus returns to earth to reign for a duration of one thousand years.

Fear of the truth

Many people have been programmed to be so negative concerning truth that, every time they hear the word "truth," they become defensive, and retort, "what is truth?" We must believe that truth will be revealed to the church on a larger scale than we ever dreamed possible. In fact, God promised truth through Christ.

- *JOH 8:31 Then said Jesus to those Jews which believed on him, If ye continue in my word, then are ye my disciples indeed; 32 And ye shall know the truth, and the truth shall make you free.*

Like-minded

One might think the author has deviated from the title and subject of this book, but this is not at all true. We are right on course. It is necessary to deal with the many divisions that have separated the children of God from one another. Especially tragic has been the mistake of dividing the church right down the middle over the matter of the baptism of the Holy Ghost and speaking with other tongues. The objective of the author is to look at why and how divisions came, and to find truth in the word of God that will unite us.

When people all believe the same truth, it unites them on that point. If allowed to do so, the Holy Spirit will teach us all the same thing.

- *ROM 15:4 For whatsoever things were written aforetime were written for our learning, that we through patience and comfort of the scriptures might have hope.*
*5 Now the God of patience and consolation grant you to be **likeminded** one toward another according to Christ Jesus:*
6 That ye may with one mind and one mouth glorify God, even the Father of our Lord Jesus Christ.
*7 **Wherefore receive ye one another, as Christ also received us to the glory of God.***

This is a New Testament command from Jesus given to the church through the apostle Paul. Such terms as *"like-minded,"* *"one mind," "one mouth," "one body,* and ***"receive ye one another,"*** are precious nuggets of truth to those who embrace the idea of unity and fellowship in the church as the one body of Christ.

Adopted sons and daughters

Rather than separating one's self from other believers over the issue of Pentecostalism, believers who know the truth about the church will rally around verse seven above, and will hold as precious truth the admonition to receive all other Christians on the basis that Christ has received them.

Paul draws an analogy of sons and daughters being adopted into a family. It is incumbent upon every child who is adopted to receive the others who have also been adopted in the same way. It is the Father's will that everyone do so. It is tragic that the family of God has been so divided while they all have been adopted into the same family by the same Father. It is not consistent with the Biblical spirit of Christianity, and yet this divided condition has been presented worldwide as the normal state of Christendom. But this will change as Christ perfects his church in the last days ... as he prepares her for the time when he will present the church to himself as a beautiful wife, at his second coming.

- *EPH 5:25 Husbands, love your wives, even as Christ also loved the church, and gave himself for it;*
  26 That he might sanctify and cleanse it with the washing of water by the word,
  27 That he might present it to himself a glorious church, not having spot, or wrinkle, or any such thing; but that it should be holy and without blemish.

The same mind

To those who love the truth regarding the Holy Spirit, scriptures such as the following will leap off the page:

- *1CO 1:10 Now I beseech you, brethren, by the name of our Lord Jesus Christ, that ye all speak the same thing, and that there be no divisions among you; but that ye be perfectly joined together **in the same mind and in the same judgment.***

The appeal for unity of faith in the church is extremely important! It is God's will that the church, as the one body of Christ, be *"perfectly joined together in the same mind and in the same judgment"* concerning the Holy Spirit. As stated earlier, the church has been split right down the middle on this issue, particularly concerning speaking in other tongues. But as the prophetic reality and fulfillment of the last days intensifies, the truth concerning the abiding of the Holy Spirit in all believers will become a treasured common denominator for the unity of the body of Christ.

This is why Paul said, *"endeavoring to keep the unity of the Spirit in the bond of peace."* It is significant that *"Spirit"* is capitalized. The phrase, *"the unity of the Spirit"* is most significant, and lets us know that the Holy Spirit is the spiritual force behind the unity of the body of Christ. The Holy Spirit will teach the same truth to all who hunger for righteousness. During the process of perfecting the saints, the Holy Spirit will not condemn division on one hand, and endorse it on the other. Neither will he teach one person one thing and teach another person something else.

Paul's next statement in support of his admonition for unity is *"There is one body* (church), *and one Spirit* (Holy Spirit), *even as ye are called in one hope of your calling"* (one heaven). This is reason enough for endeavoring to *"keep the unity of the Spirit in the bond of peace"* (Christ's love).

Start by stopping

A good starting place could be for the entire body of Christ to discontinue the practice of designating themselves as Pentecostal or Non-Pentecostal. It is incumbent upon both sides to discover common ground in the scripture that will bring both factions into one union with God through truth found only in the word of God, and not in the traditions of either side.

Many will jump at the chance to refute this by saying, "you will never find two men who see exactly alike." This may be true in a natural sense, but the Holy Spirit will be able to find many who see alike on spiritual things ... as he teaches them all the same thing. We already have a great starting point, for there are millions who already see alike concerning Jesus -- who he is, what he is, and what he will do. Our common ground is Jesus. We are commanded -- based on the name of Jesus -- to *"all speak the same thing."*

- *1CO 1:10 Now I beseech you, brethren, by the name of <u>our Lord Jesus Christ</u>, that ye all speak the same thing, and that there be no divisions among you; but that ye perfectly joined together in the same mind and in the same judgment.*

This common ground can be found only in the scripture as we are all taught the same thing ... by the Holy Spirit. If one looks anywhere else other than the scripture they will not find it. This is what Jesus said the Holy Spirit would do; *"he shall guide you into all truth."* The natural mind says this is impossible, but one must not be controlled by the natural mind ... which is classified by Scripture as the "carnal mind," which is *"the spirit of the world."*

- *1CO 2:12 Now we have received, not the spirit of the world, but the spirit which is of God; that we might know the things that are freely given to us of God.*
  13 Which things also we speak, not in the words which man's wisdom teacheth, but which the Holy Ghost teacheth; comparing spiritual things with spiritual.
  14 But the natural man receiveth not the things of the Spirit of God: for they are foolishness unto him: neither can he know them, because they are spiritually discerned.

All must use the spiritual mind which was given when they were *"born of the Spirit,"* ... at the time of their new birth.

They that understand shall instruct many

Daniel saw people who would instruct others in the last days. It is not too much for one to hope to be one of those instructors? Being a pioneer for truth is not easy ... and has never been easy. But, it is worth it if one understands the truth regarding the Holy Spirit, and can share it with others.

- *DAN 11:32 ... but the people that do know their God shall be strong, and do exploits.*
  33 And they that understand among the people shall instruct many:

Just think about what is happening when one claims to be non-Pentecostal, which means they discard a major portion of the Bible. That portion has to do with scriptural information concerning important Holy Ghost truth relating to God's major **Gift** which he gave to all believers on the day of Pentecost.

- *ACT 2:1 And when the day of Pentecost was fully come, they were all with one accord in one place.*
  *2 And suddenly there came a sound **from heaven** as of a rushing mighty wind, and it filled all the house where they were sitting.*
  3 And there appeared unto them cloven tongues like as of fire, and it sat upon each of them.
  4 And they were all filled with the Holy Ghost, and began to speak with other tongues, as the Spirit gave them utterance.
- *ACT 2:38 Then Peter said unto them, Repent, and be baptized every one of you in the name of Jesus Christ for the remission of sins, and ye shall receive the **gift of the Holy Ghost**.*
  39 For the promise is unto you, and to your children, and to all that are afar off, <u>even as many as the Lord our God shall call.</u> (To every person who is saved).

4

Unity of the Spirit

The author sincerely believes his prayerful fifty-five year study of issues that have divided God's people, has led him into understanding Biblical truth that can be welcomed by both sides. As has been stated, a major cause for disunity has been over the matter of the gift of tongues. Granted, many Christians claim to be filled with the Holy Spirit, yet they omit most manifestations of the gifts of the Spirit, including speaking in other tongues.

The most pronounced division within Christianity is between Pentecostals and Non-Pentecostals. It seems appropriate that this should be a major area for striving for unity? Paul called upon the church to humbly demonstrate meekness toward one another, putting forth an extreme effort (endeavoring) to maintain the unity of the Spirit. Paul made his appeal on the basis that there is only *"one body"* (the one church), and *"one Spirit,"* meaning *"one Holy Spirit.* Paul added *"one hope of your calling,"* (meaning *Heaven*), plus other important *"ones."* All these *"ones"* should be reason enough to unite believers in the *"one faith"* under the *"one Lord"* and the *"one God"* who is the *"one Father"* of all his spiritual family. Here are the exact words of Paul:

- *EPH 4:4 There is one body, and one Spirit, even as ye are called in one hope of your calling;*
  5 One Lord, __one faith__, one baptism,
  6 One God and Father of all, who is above all, and through all, and in you all.

It is high time that all of Christendom be confronted over the factions regarding the Holy Spirit. Both sides have held part of the truth and it seems that never the twain should meet, but this cannot continue to apply to children of the same heavenly Father, and who are in the same body, his church.

One body

Paul makes an appeal for unity by pointing out that every member in the body of Christ has the same Holy Spirit, and it is this one-and-only Spirit that places all believers into the one-and-only church ... the body of Christ.

- *1CO 12:13 For by one Spirit are we all baptized into one body, whether we be Jews or Gentiles, whether we be bond or free; and have been all made to drink into one Spirit.*
  14 For the body is not one member, but many.

Just as the members of our human body -- hands, feet, eyes, ears, etc. -- are interconnected into one unit, so is the church with all its members. If my hand claimed it was not a part of my body, or claimed to be a part of some other body, it would not make it so.

Paul said he suffered the loss of all things, which included all his Jewish background and traditions in order to gain the excellent knowledge of Christ.

- *PHI 3:8 Yea doubtless, and I count all things but loss for the excellency of the knowledge of Christ Jesus my Lord: for whom I have suffered the loss of all things, and do count them but dung, that I may win Christ,*

Today the vast majority of Christians believe traditions rooted mainly in Non-Pentecostal denominational doctrines. Regardless of how powerful they are, Non-Pentecostal traditions are giving way to the unity of the Spirit which is working in the church today throughout the world. A few decades back many people in formal and traditional nominal churches had little or no knowledge about the Holy Spirit because they rarely heard any mention of him from the pulpit in their church. But with the advent of the Charismatic movement many people right in their midst began broaching the subject, and the exposure to the subject has been effective. Today many more references are being heard regarding the Holy Spirit, even from their pulpits. Non-Charismatics in defense began to claim to be filled with the Holy Spirit while discounting speaking in other tongues.

A vast majority of Christians have believed only those things which have come forth from man's wisdom, but as these things are rectified through the truth that the Holy Ghost teaches, drastic changes are coming about within Christianity.

- *1CO 2:13 Which things also we speak, not in the words which man's wisdom teacheth, but which the Holy Ghost teacheth; comparing spiritual things with spiritual.*

It is imperative that we think of the Holy Spirit as the teacher of truth, and as the promoter of unity within the body of Christ. All of his ministries are important. If we can emphasize the unity of the brotherhood, we will see the Holy Spirit manifesting himself greatly within that fellowship of love. Doctrinal antagonism prevents the full and free flowing of the Spirit as the anointing oil of God.

We must think of the Biblical church strictly within scriptural guidelines, and not in terms of its traditional present-day divided format. We must strive for unity within this body, and hold fast to the fact that Jesus has only one church. He said, "my church" and it is evident he has only one. Paul asked the question, "*is Christ divided?*" meaning, is Christ the head over two or more bodies (1CO 1:13)? One must get beyond believing doctrines based on what "their church" believes. Hearing Jesus say, "*my church*" will become increasingly endearing.

This writing is not grinding a Pentecostal axe, neither is it attacking Non-Pentecostal believers, but is preaching the unity of the body of Christ. The light of truth must shine into every crevasse of the church. That which is not sound doctrine must be manifested by the light.

- *EPH 5:13 But all things that are reproved are made manifest by the light: for whatsoever doth make manifest is light.*
  14 Wherefore he saith, Awake thou that sleepest, and arise from the dead, and Christ shall give thee light.

The truth is, the division that exists within the ranks of Christianity today is soundly condemned by the word of God. In spite of this, many are very optimistic about the future of the church. There is more common ground within professing Christianity than one might think.

While I strongly believe the terms *Pentecostal* and *Non-Pentecostal* are Biblical misnomers, I use them reluctantly in this book because they have become coined words in our religious vernacular, and for the purpose of exposing their divisive connotation. The very fact their normal use is scripturally unsound and divisive should let us know that something is wrong and out of order.

I actually feel a sense of guilt if I refer to myself as a Pentecostal, because I am admitting to being different from some others in the family of God; or saying that some believers are different from me. I refrain from using the terms in normal conversation, but for purposes set forth in this book, I cannot deny the strong doctrinal differences which are implied by each term. I want to magnify the erroneous idea behind the reasons that some believers identify themselves as Pentecostal while others as Non-Pentecostal. This does not conform to the truth that there is only one faith. This idea did not come from the gospel of Christ.

- *PHI 1:27 Only let your conversation be as it becometh the gospel of Christ: that whether I come and see you, or else be absent, I may hear of your affairs, that ye stand fast in one spirit, with one mind striving together for the faith of the gospel;*
- *PHI 2:2 Fulfil ye my joy, that ye be likeminded, having the same love, being of one accord, of one mind.*

Many believers are discarding the practice of referring to themselves as Pentecostal because they see that it is a designator which divides brethren. By the same token, believers must discontinue referring to themselves as Non-Pentecostal. To the Jews, Pentecost meant the fiftieth day after Passover. It was on this Jewish feast day that the Holy Ghost fell on the church.

The term "Pentecostal" has come to mean "I believe in the Holy Ghost just as he came on the day of Pentecost, complete with speaking in other tongues." "Non-Pentecostal" has come to mean "I believe in the Holy Ghost just as he came on the day of Pentecost, except that tongues are not for the church today."

Baptism in the Spirit at the time of the new birth

Most who call themselves "Non-Pentecostals" believe they receive the Holy Ghost when they get saved, but, for the most part, they shy away from any literal operation, or manifestation of the gifts of the Holy Spirit in their life personally, or in their church ... frequently implying that the supernatural gifts are no longer operative in the church.

The important truth regarding this matter is that all believers should find unity in knowing they are all Christians, and should stay away from calling themselves Pentecostal Christians or Non-Pentecostal Christians.

The word *"Christian"* is a powerful Biblical identifier.

- *ACT 11:26 ... And it came to pass, that a whole year they assembled themselves with the church, and taught much people. And the disciples were called **Christians** first in Antioch.*

Tongues as the initial evidence

As it stands today, those who identify themselves as "Pentecostals" believe that one does not receive the baptism of the Holy Ghost until such time as one speaks in other tongues, which is said to be "the initial evidence" that the Holy Ghost has taken up residence within a believer.

The baptism with the Holy Ghost is believed by Pentecostals to be an experience, separate from, and subsequent to the experience of obtaining salvation. It is accepted that both experiences can, and might, occur within practically the same time frame, or the same prayer session, but are two distinctly separate experiences. These opinions will be explored in depth before we are through.

One faith

Since the Bible teaches there is only one Father, only one Jesus, one Holy Ghost, one heaven, one church and one faith, let's believe that God can lead us all into that one faith concerning the Holy Spirit.

There must be a central truth hidden somewhere within the scripture that will bring the church into unity on this issue. Let's go on a treasure hunt together. Treasures we will hope to uncover scripturally are answers to the following questions: "Does one receive the Holy Ghost when they are saved"? "Do all speak in tongues"? "Is speaking in other tongues the initial evidence of receiving the Holy Ghost"? "Has speaking in tongues ceased"? "Are *other tongues* speaking of actual human languages," known and spoken somewhere in the world?

You Shall Receive

Let's attempt to settle the issue now. Does one receive the gift of the Holy Ghost when they are born again, meaning when they are saved and placed into Christ … which Paul describes as being *"baptized into Christ?"* It is <u>at the moment when one receives *"remission of sins"* that they also *"receive the gift of the Holy Ghost."*</u>

- *ACT 2:38 Then Peter said unto them, Repent, and be baptized every one of you in the name of Jesus Christ for the remission of sins, and <u>ye shall receive the gift of the Holy Ghost</u>.*
  39 For the promise is unto you, and to your children, and to all that are afar off, even as many as the Lord our God shall call.

This is indispensable information!!! When one truly "repents" they are "Baptized into Christ," which means "placed into Christ." According to verse 38, at the time of genuine repentance, God forgives their sins, baptizes them into Christ, and gives them the gift of the Holy Ghost.

After That Ye Believed

AFTER one becomes a believer in Christ, and **AFTER** they repent for their sins, without delay, God responds to that faith by forgiving their sins, and by placing them into Christ, and **by giving them the promised gift of the Holy Ghost**.

- *EPH 1:13 In whom ye also trusted, **after** that ye heard the word of truth, the gospel of your salvation: in whom also **AFTER** that ye believed, ye were sealed with that holy Spirit of **promise**,*
  14 Which is the earnest of our inheritance until the redemption of the purchased possession, unto the praise of his glory.

SUMMARY: AS A PART OF THE NEW BIRTH, ONE RECEIVES THE GIFT OF THE HOLY SPIRIT AS A MAJOR COMPLETION AND CONFIRMATION OF THE SALVATION PROCESS. (Memorize ACTS 2:38.)

- *ACT 2:38 Then Peter said unto them, Repent, and be baptized every one of you in the name of Jesus Christ for the remission of sins, and ye shall receive the gift of the Holy Ghost.*

THREE BAPTISMS

The New Testament gives reference to three separate baptisms which are, **"Baptism in Water," "Baptism into Christ,"** and **"Baptism with the Holy Ghost."**

Baptism in Water began with the ministry of John the Baptist. The term "Baptism" means "to be placed into," or "immersed into." Water baptism is an action of obedience taken by man, and is symbolic of the spiritual conversion whereby the spiritual man of a convert to Christ has been completely submerged, or baptized into Christ by total submission to him as their Lord and Savior. Baptism in water is a personal declaration of total faith that Jesus has power and authority from God to forgive sins, to cleanse and wash from the human carnal sinful nature, and to give the promise of eternal life in heaven.

God requires **Repentance for sins** prior to baptism in Water.

* *MAT 3:7 But when he saw many of the Pharisees and Sadducees come to his baptism, he said unto them, O generation of vipers, who hath warned you to flee from the wrath to come?*
  8 Bring forth therefore fruits meet for repentance:

Baptism into Christ is the first essential baptism which comes from God, and must precede Baptism in Water. Obtaining Baptism into Christ means that one has become a firm believer in Christ, and they have become a disciple and follower of Christ's Gospel message. In his omnipresence Christ becomes resident within their body, and mind, and spirit. Baptism into Christ is a dual immersion whereby a believer is placed into Christ, and Christ is placed within them.

- *JOH 15:5 I am the vine, ye are the branches: He that <u>abideth in me</u>, and <u>I in him</u>, the same bringeth forth much fruit: for without me ye can do nothing.*

Baptism in the Holy Ghost

Repentance and baptism into Christ is required by God as a prerequisite before he will baptize in the Holy Ghost.

- *ACT 2:38 Then Peter said unto them, Repent, and be baptized every one of you <u>in the name of Jesus Christ</u> (which is baptism into Christ) for the remission of sins, and ye shall receive the gift of the Holy Ghost.*

The Holy Ghost is **promised** to everyone who responds to God's call to salvation and who becomes a child of God.

- *ACT 2:39 For the promise is unto you, and to your children, and to all that are afar off, even as many as the Lord our God shall call.*

At this point I will say quite a bit about the Holy Ghost. Every Christian should believe and experience the Baptism in the Holy Ghost because Jesus believed and taught it by saying,

- *ACT 1:5 For John truly baptized with water; but ye shall be baptized with the Holy Ghost not many days hence.*

Baptism in the Holy Ghost is not a second or third work of grace, as has been taught by Pentecostalism, but is a baptism given by God to believers when they are saved. Baptism in the Holy Ghost is a vital part of the salvation process that occurs when one is saved. This is an important truth thoroughly discussed in this book, and answers the question concerning "**when**" one is given the gift of the Holy Spirit.

A common teaching among Pentecostals is that, one can be saved at the time of their initial conversion, but may not receive the gift of the Holy Ghost at that time. A frequent Pentecostal experience is that, after a length of time, often after prolonged tarrying and seeking, they will eventually receive the Baptism in the Holy Ghost, and will speak in other tongues as the **initial evidence** that the Holy Spirit has finally been given to them.

The **initial evidence** is not the corresponding moment when one speaks in tongues for the first time. The initial evidence is that which is spoken by the Bible, which is Word from God, and is the **initial evidence** which declares that the Holy Spirit comes into a believer when they are saved. The **initial evidence** of Biblical truth is that, **when one is saved God gives them the gift of the Holy Ghost.** Every sincere believer in Jesus must accept this truth of God which says,

- *ACT 2:38 ... Repent, and be baptized every one of you in the name of Jesus Christ for the remission of sins, and "YE SHALL RECEIVE" the gift of the Holy Ghost. 39 For the promise is unto you, and to your children, and to all that are afar off, even as many as the Lord our God shall call.*

Mark the words in your Bible, **"Ye SHALL receive,"** with "**SHALL**" in bold caps and underlined.

Gifts of the Holy Spirit

The Bible also includes information regarding **"gifts"** of the Holy Spirit. These spiritual gifts accompany the indwelling of the Holy Spirit.

Every person who is saved should also accept information given in the Bible concerning the **gifts of the Spirit**. A listing of nine gifts of the Spirit is given in bold type in the following passage:

- *1CO 12:8 For to one is given by the Spirit the **word of wisdom**; to another the **word of knowledge** by the same Spirit;*
  *9 To another **faith** by the same Spirit; to another the **gifts of healing** by the same Spirit;*
  *10 To another the **working of miracles**; to another **prophecy**; to another **discerning of spirits**; to another **divers kinds of tongues** (various kinds of languages); to another the **interpretation of tongues**:*
  11 But all these worketh that one and the selfsame Spirit, dividing to every man severally as he will.

Of these gifts, speaking in other tongues is given to all receivers as confirmation that the Holy Ghost is indwelling them. Every person who is saved by the grace of God should believe through faith that they received the gift of the Holy Ghost when they were saved. Therefore, they should expect that the indwelling Holy Spirit will manifest his presence through them as revealed in the Bible.

Speaking in Other Tongues

Biblical truth concerning the indwelling of the Holy Ghost also includes information concerning the gift of **"Speaking in other tongues"** (other languages), which is not done by the person speaking, but is done by the **"utterance"** of the indwelling Holy Spirit. This first occurred when the Holy Ghost was given on the day of Pentecost.

- *ACT 2:4 And they were all filled with the Holy Ghost, and began to speak with other tongues, <u>as the Spirit gave them utterance.</u>*

Every Christian believer should experience Speaking in other tongues by the utterance of the Holy Spirit because it is thoroughly and totally Biblical.

Nine Gifts of the Holy Spirit were given by God when the Holy Ghost was **poured out**, and Speaking in Tongues was one of those gifts.

- *ACT 10:45 And they of the circumcision which believed were astonished, as many as came with Peter, because that on the Gentiles also was <u>poured out</u> the gift of the Holy Ghost.*
  46 For they heard them speak with tongues, and magnify God.

It is important to believe that the promises of Christ should be fulfilled within those who believe in Christ, who said the following:

- *ACT 1:8 But ye shall receive power, after that the Holy Ghost is come upon you: and ye shall be witnesses unto me both in Jerusalem, and in all Judaea, and in Samaria, and unto the uttermost part of the earth.*

It is sad that many Christians have existed in doctrinal environments that have blinded their spiritual eyes and mind to the Biblical truth concerning the Holy Ghost which Jesus understood and knew, and taught very well. Therefore everyone who is seeking to please Christ should pray to God that they will be given **the mind of Christ** as they experience the fulfillment of his promises concerning the gifts of the Holy Spirit.

- *1CO 2:16 For who hath known the mind of the Lord, that he may instruct him? <u>But we have the mind of Christ</u>.*

I rejoice to say that, according to Google on the internet, a phenomenal worldwide interest and religious awakening concerning the Holy Spirit is occurring today. And, **by far the largest area of statistical growth within Christianity involves a thriving movement toward faith in the promised gifts of Christ regarding the Holy Spirit.** This is already beginning to happen.

PENTECOSTAL GROWTH WORLD-WIDE

The internet has many articles by outstanding authors giving information regarding Pentecostal Growth World-wide.

The tremendous world-wide interest in the Holy Spirit that has developed in America, as well as throughout the world is amazing. Mutual agreement comes from the opinions of religious scholars that the late 20th century will probably be known as the era of the "Pentecostal Explosion."

A notable summary is, "The sheer speed of growth of Pentecostal and Charismatic Christianity is difficult to exaggerate. In the late 1990's the number of Spirit filled believers had grown to over 410 million, and amounted to 24.2 percent of world Christianity. By now those figures have grown exponentially.

Some expositors regarding the Pentecostal Explosion have concluded that in all human history, no other voluntary human movement has grown as rapidly as the Pentecostal-Charismatic movement in the last 25 years.

One of the latest and largest estimates of the number of global Pentecostal and Charismatic Christians, according to a 2006 statement, is that there are now six hundred million Pentecostal and Charismatic Christians in the world, which is more than one quarter of all Christians in the world. The effect of this explosion is so significant that religious statisticians say that the Pentecostal expansion has been so astonishing as to justify claims of a new Reformation.

The Pentecostal and Charismatic Identification refers to Christians who believe and support and practice that God has placed the gift of the Holy Ghost to dwell in their body, such as occurred on the day of Pentecost.

- *1CO 6:19 What? know ye not that your body is the temple of the Holy Ghost which is in you, which ye have of God, and ye are not your own?*
  20 For ye are bought with a price: therefore glorify God in your body, and in your spirit, which are God's.

According to the Bible, in the last days, just prior to the second coming of Christ, there will be a major world-wide outpouring of the Holy Spirit. This is already beginning to happen.

- *ACT 2:17 And it shall come to pass in the last days, saith God, I will pour out of my Spirit upon all flesh: and your sons and your daughters shall prophesy, and your young men shall see visions, and your old men shall dream dreams:*
  18 And on my servants and on my handmaidens <u>I will pour out in those days of my Spirit</u>; and they shall prophesy:

Through scriptural reference we know that the Spirit which God "pours out" is the Holy Ghost.

- *ACT 10:45 … because that on the Gentiles also was <u>poured out the gift of the Holy Ghost.</u>*
  46 For they heard them speak with tongues, and magnify God.

Every saved person should believe everything God says in his Word regarding the Holy Ghost. Every Christian believer should experience Speaking in other tongues by the utterance of the Holy Spirit because it is thoroughly and totally Biblical.

For many people the matter regarding the Holy Ghost is not that it is a Biblical matter, but to them it is a matter which they want to believe, or is a matter they <u>do not</u> want to believe. The power of choice regarding obeying God concerning the Holy Spirit is under their individual control.

- *JOS 24:15 … <u>choose you this day whom ye will serve;</u> … <u>but as for me and my house, we will serve the LORD</u>.*

I choose to believe everything God says in his Holy Word **"ABOUT THE HOLY SPIRIT,"** which is the title of this book.

5

Other Tongues (Languages)

This is an extremely important chapter in this book. It contains a large volume of scriptural references. The spiritual life of anyone who is striving to live by faith in God and in Jesus must be aware of an absolute truth. That truth is, one must live their daily life according to the word of God.

- *MAT 4:3 And when the tempter came to him, he said, If thou be the Son of God, command that these stones be made bread. 4 But he answered and said, It is written, Man shall not live by bread alone, but by every word that proceedeth out of the mouth of God.*

The word of God is recorded in the Bible which is a miraculous treasure and storehouse of truth which has been given to mankind by God himself. This chapter five contains many words from God regarding one of the most vital subjects given by God. That subject pertains to information ABOUT THE HOLY SPIRIT, which is the title on the front of this book.

I encourage each reader to closely analyze every statement, and especially every scripture presented on the pages of this book. Jesus said that man shall live by "**every word of God.**" This means that **all** words of God must be taken seriously. This book you are reading contains serious words from God regarding speaking in tongues. To *"speak with other tongues"* is a Biblical phrase … meaning "a word of God phrase." The next Biblical reference is a "word of God phrase."

- *ACT 2:4 And they were all filled with the Holy Ghost, and began to <u>speak with other tongues</u> as the Spirit gave them utterance.*

Speaking with other tongues is one of nine gifts of the Holy Spirit named in the twelfth chapter of First Corinthians. It means to speak by supernatural utterance in a language unknown to the person speaking … but is a valid foreign language (another tongue) spoken and understood somewhere in the world.

Scriptural proof that speaking in tongues is speaking in foreign languages can be found in the following passage:

- *ACT 2:5 And there were dwelling at Jerusalem Jews, devout men, out of every nation under heaven.*
  *6 Now when this was noised abroad, the multitude came together, and were confounded, because that every man heard them speak in his own **<u>language</u>**.*
  7 And they were all amazed and marvelled, saying one to another, Behold, are not all these which speak Galilaeans?
  *8 And how hear we every man in our own **<u>tongue</u>**, wherein we were born?*

Languages from fifteen different nations are listed.

- *ACT 2:8 And how hear we every man in our own tongue, wherein we were born?*

9 Parthians, and Medes, and Elamites, and the dwellers in Mesopotamia, and in Judaea, and Cappadocia, in Pontus, and Asia,

10 Phrygia, and Pamphylia, in Egypt, and in the parts of Libya about Cyrene, and strangers of Rome, Jews and proselytes,

11 Cretes and Arabians, we do hear them speak in our tongues the wonderful works of God.

12 And they were all amazed, and were in doubt, saying one to another, What meaneth this?

Speaking in other tongues was one of the supernatural gifts manifested on the day of Pentecost when the divine person, the Holy Ghost, also called the Holy Spirit, came to live in omnipresence within each individual born again Christian.

Jesus shall baptize you

The matter of the Holy Ghost has profound doctrinal importance. John the Baptist was sent by God to be the forerunner of Christ, and he introduced Jesus as the Son of God. He also introduced Jesus as the one who would baptize with the Holy Ghost. John the Baptist had this knowledge because God himself had told him.

God had revealed many things to John, by direct conversations with him. John knew he would baptize the Messiah in water. He also knew that when he baptize him, the Holy Ghost would come upon the Messiah to empower him for his earthly ministry.

- *John 1:33 And I knew him not: but he that sent me to baptize with water, the same said unto me, Upon whom thou shalt see the Spirit descending, and remaining on him, <u>the same is he which baptizeth with the Holy Ghost</u>.*

If God instructed John the Baptist to introduce Jesus as the one who would baptize in the Holy Ghost, it must be important, and worthy of our special attention. Those who have given little attention to the Holy Ghost should seriously consider this matter as worthy of special Biblical attention.

- *HEB 2:1 Therefore we ought to give the more earnest heed to the things which we have heard, lest at any time we should let them slip.*

If one does not seriously ponder Biblically this matter of speaking in other tongues, it can slip away in spite of what the Bible says about it. It is a serious matter when a person hears what God says regarding the reality of the Holy Spirit and speaking in other tongues, and they push it into the back of their mind, wanting to ignore, or forget it, or oppose it.

- *JAM 1:22 But be ye doers of the word, and not hearers only, deceiving your own selves.*
  23 For if any be a hearer of the word, and not a doer, he is like unto a man beholding his natural face in a glass:
  24 For he beholdeth himself, and goeth his way, and straightway forgetteth what manner of man he was.
  25 But whoso looketh into the perfect law of liberty, and continueth therein, he being not a forgetful hearer, but a doer of the work, this man shall be blessed in his deed.

Many who can testify regarding the fullness of the Holy Spirit will attest to the fact that by walking in that truth they have been blessed thereby. Verse 25 above says, "whoever continueth as a doer shall be blessed."

Born of the Spirit

A careful study of the ministry of Christ reveals that he came to earth to accomplish many things. One of these important things was that he would provide the means, through his death and resurrection, whereby men could be reconciled to God. The Holy Spirit would become the force from God which would enter into man, regenerating him into a new creature in Christ Jesus ... born again ... born of the Spirit. It is by the infilling of the Spirit that one is born again. This is exactly what Jesus explained to Nicodemus.

- *JOH 3:6 That which is born of the flesh is flesh;and that which is born of the Spirit is spirit.*
  7 Marvel not that I said unto thee, Ye must be born again.

At what precise moment does the Holy Spirit take up his abode within a newly born again believer in Christ? This is the crux issue. Before the Holy Ghost was given on the day of Pentecost, Jesus told his disciples the Holy Ghost was *"with"* them, but the time would come when he would be *"in"* them. When does he come in?

- *JOH 14:17 Even the Spirit of truth; whom the world cannot receive, because it seeth him not, neither knoweth him: but ye know him; for he dwelleth <u>with</u> you, and shall be <u>in</u> you.*

At the time Jesus spoke this, The Holy Spirit was dwelling within *Jesus*. The disciples had not received the Holy Ghost as an indwelling Spirit, and he only dwelled *"with"* them at that present time. The Holy Spirit was with them in the fact that he was *"in"* Christ who was with them. He was also with them as only an outside force, but would soon take up his abode "within" them as a dynamic abiding spiritual force. This was confirmed in the book of Acts.

- *ACT 2:4 And they were all __filled__ with the Holy Ghost, and began to speak with other tongues, as the Spirit gave them utterance.*

Notice that they were *"__all__ filled with the Holy Ghost."* Jesus said the Holy Ghost would be a teacher and guide that would lead those who received him into **all** truth. Many years after the day of Pentecost John had this to say:

- *1JO 2:27 But the anointing which ye have received of him abideth in you, and ye need not that any man teach you: but as the same anointing teacheth you of all things, and is truth, and is no lie, and even as it hath taught you, ye shall abide in him.*

The Holy Spirit is involved in all phases of one's spiritual relationship with God, from the very first sense of conviction for sin ... all the way through conversion ... and the subsequent life and walk in the Spirit. The Holy Spirit is involved from the very beginning of the process of salvation by reproving of sin. This is how conviction for sin occurs.

- *JOH 16:8 And when he is come, he will reprove the world of sin, and of righteousness, and of judgment:*

Born of the Spirit

The Holy Spirit gives the power and anointing by which one is born again. He works with Jesus Christ and God the Father in all he does. The Holy Spirit is so intimately involved that the Bible says when one is saved, they are "**born of the Spirit**."

- *JOH 3:6 That which is born of the flesh is flesh; and that which is **born of the Spirit** is spirit.*
  7 Marvel not that I said unto thee, Ye must be born again.
  *8 The wind bloweth where it listeth, and thou hearest the sound thereof, but canst not tell whence it cometh, and whither it goeth: so is every one that is **born of the Spirit**.*

When a person is born again, their new birth is accomplished by the Holy Spirit, even for those who claim to be Non-Pentecostal. Jesus said, *"so is everyone that is born of the Spirit." (John 3:8).* Encounters with the Holy Spirit are unavoidable for everyone who has been born again. Every Spirit-filled Christian should openly and freely acknowledge the Holy Spirit.

Instead of claiming to be Non-Pentecostal, it would be Biblically advisable to change that introduction by saying, "I am a born again Christian. When I was saved, I was *born of the Spirit*" (JOH 3:8)."

Jesus became our example in all things, especially concerning being filled with the Spirit. If it was necessary for Jesus in his humanity as an ordinary man to be empowered by the Holy Spirit in order to do his ministry, how much more important is it for us today?

- *ACT 10:38 How God anointed Jesus of Nazareth with the Holy Ghost and with power: who went about doing good, and healing all that were oppressed of the devil; for God was with him.*

Fell on them

God said to John the Baptist concerning Jesus, *"Upon whom thou shalt see the Spirit descending, and remaining on him."* The coming down of the Holy Spirit from heaven also occurred at Cornelius' house.

While Peter was preaching about *"how God anointed Jesus of Nazareth with the Holy Ghost,* the Holy Ghost *"fell on all them which heard the word."*

- *ACT 10:44 While Peter yet spake these words, the Holy Ghost fell on all them which heard the word.*
  45 And they of the circumcision which believed were astonished, as many as came with Peter, because that on the Gentiles also was poured out the gift of the Holy Ghost.
  46 For they heard them speak with tongues, and magnify God,

Remained on them

This is an exact parallel of what happened to Jesus in the Jordan River, where it says that the Spirit *"remained on him."* Jesus told his disciples the Holy Ghost would *"abide with them forever"* (JOH 14:16).

Saved but not baptized in the Spirit

Today It is traditionally taught by most Pentecostals that one can be saved without receiving the Holy Spirit. It is contended that this is what happens to Non-Pentecostals who do not embrace the entire Pentecostal doctrine including speaking in other tongues. It is also believed that this is what happens to all who are born again (meaning saved) but do not speak in other tongues.

The above is primarily how the Pentecostal and Non-Pentecostal theologies stand currently and are presented to the world today.

I hope the reader of this book will take a fresh look with me at the matter of the timing of the incoming of the Holy Spirit, to see if there is not some room for improvement in Biblical interpretation on both sides. It is believed that a fresh study of this subject can be beneficial in uniting the two distinctly divided theological groups.

The theme of this book entitled "ABOUT THE HOLY SPIRIT" will be placed in short statements, and then we will go into detail to show the scriptural proof of that which is stated.

Statement No. 1. The Holy Ghost is given to every believer at the time of the new birth ... immediately upon God's acceptance of their acknowledgment of Christ through confession and repentance.

When God is satisfied with their sincere approach to him through Jesus as their Mediator, Redeemer, Savior and Lord, he forgives them, washes away their sins by the blood of Jesus, regenerates them into new creatures, places them into Christ, adds them to his family – which is the church -- and places the Holy Spirit within them immediately and without fail.

The Spirit becomes their comforter, guide, teacher, reprover, and empowers them for Christian life and service in the kingdom of God.

Statement No. 2. The gift of the Holy Spirit is God's initial response to one's confession, repentance, and declared faith in Christ. The Holy Ghost is given to believers as God's sign, or proof that he has received them into his family.

Statement No. 3. When a person decides to receive Christ, they must acknowledge by faith that Christ has come into their heart.

Statement No. 4. They should believe the promise that Christ has given them the Holy Spirit.

Statement No. 5. The indwelling of the Holy Spirit gives every believer the potential for the manifestation of all fruit of the Spirit and all the gifts of the Spirit including speaking in other tongues.

The above Statements should be preached, and taught, and evangelized, and proclaimed, and indoctrinated into the hearts, and minds, and spirits, and memories of the world, to every prospective convert to Christ.

Truth must be well planted about the full abiding and indwelling of the Holy Spirit as a gift of God to everyone who believes in Christ, and receives the Holy Spirit into their being ... soul and body ... heart and mind ... by faith. This should be included in the messages of salvation proclaimed by the body of Christ ... which is his church.

Meet for repentance

John the Baptist introduced the New Testament plan of salvation which would come through Christ. He preached that one must first bring forth fruit *"meet for"* repentance, and the consequence would be that Jesus would baptize them with the Holy Ghost. It is significant to note that Jesus was introduced as the baptizer in the Holy Ghost.

"Meet for" means "sufficient for" or "meeting the requirement." God knows whether or not one's repentance is sincere, and if one's sorrow for sin is genuine. God knows the thoughts and intents of the heart, and only God knows when repentance meets his requirements according to his plan of justification and redemption.

- *MAT 3:8 Bring forth therefore fruits meet for repentance:*
  9 And think not to say within yourselves, We have Abraham to our father: for I say unto you, that God is able of these stones to raise up children unto Abraham.
  10 And now also the axe is laid unto the root of the trees: therefore every tree which bringeth not forth good fruit is hewn down, and cast into the fire.

This new plan of salvation by grace through faith in Christ applies to all men. The Jews could no longer boast of any special advantage with God because they were descendants of Abraham. Religious pride would be a hindrance in this new dispensation of grace.

Christ's response to repentance

- *MAT 3:11 I indeed baptize you with water unto repentance: but he that cometh after me is mightier than I, whose shoes I am not worthy to bear: he shall baptize you with the Holy Ghost, and with fire:*

John's baptism (immersion) in water was symbolic of repentance (changing directions), dramatically portraying the process of the death, burial, and resurrection of Christ, which every sinner must literally experience in their own life. Repentance and the new birth, are not speaking of an experience which is brought about by water baptism, but refers to a "spiritual" baptism which must occur before water baptism is celebrated. This spiritual baptism is elsewhere called the *"new birth"* which was also called *"being born of the Spirit,"* *"baptized into Christ,"* and *"born again."*

Saved

One would have difficulty Biblically in attempting to separate the salvation experience from being baptized in the Holy Spirit. What does it mean to be saved? This was the reason for which Jesus came into the world.

- *LUK 19:10 For the Son of man is come to seek and to **save** that which was lost.*

Paul and Silas were imprisoned in Philippi. God sent an earthquake and set them free. The jailer thought everyone had escaped and was about to take his own life when Paul let him know they were all there. The jailer knew God had done this and was so convicted he wanted to get saved right then. Notice his question concerning how to be saved. Also notice carefully Paul's answer.

- *ACT 16:29 Then he called for a light, and sprang in, and came trembling, and fell down before Paul and Silas,*
  30 And brought them out, and said, Sirs, what must I do to be saved?
  31 And they said, Believe on the Lord Jesus Christ, and thou shalt be saved, and thy house.

When one truly believes on the Lord Jesus Christ, the Savior immediately accomplishes his saving work in response to their believing by placing the Holy Ghost within them. This is termed a baptism in the Holy Ghost, and is called "being born of the **Spirit**."

One is saved as a result of believing on the Lord Jesus Christ. One is also baptized in the Holy Ghost through believing on Jesus.

This is why Paul's question to the disciples of John the Baptist in Ephesus is so significant.

- *ACT 19:2 He said unto them, Have ye received the Holy Ghost since ye believed?*

Today it should be expected that anyone who truly believes in Jesus receives the Holy Spirit as God's response to this believing. All aspects of regeneration and the new birth are accomplished by the acts and ministry of the Holy Spirit as he applies Christ's provisions through his life, death, burial, resurrection, ascension, and intercession. Jesus most definitely told Nicodemus that being born again was a work of the Spirit.

- *JOH 3:7 Marvel not that I said unto thee, Ye must be born again.*
  *8 The wind bloweth where it listeth, and thou hearest the sound thereof, but canst not tell whence it cometh, and whither it goeth: so is every one that is **born of the Spirit**.*

Ten days after Christ had ascended back to heaven, God sent the Holy Spirit from heaven to the church. The divine purpose for the coming of the Holy Spirit was that he might indwell <u>all</u> believers. The Holy Spirit would administer all the benefits of Christ to those who believed on him, and the salvation process would be realized by each individual as the Holy Spirit magnified Christ to them. This gift of the Holy Spirit was "***<u>abundantly</u>***" shared from God through Christ.

- *TIT 3:5 Not by works of righteousness which we have done, but according to his mercy **<u>he saved us</u>**, by the washing of regeneration, and **<u>renewing of the Holy Ghost</u>**;*

6 Which he shed on us <u>abundantly</u> through Jesus Christ our Saviour;
*7 That being <u>**justified**</u> by his grace, we should be <u>**made heirs**</u> according to the hope of eternal life.*

The above scripture is one of the most convincing that the gift of the Holy Ghost is received when Christ saves us, at which time we are justified by his grace, and we become heirs according to the hope of eternal life.

Every person who claims to be saved, but has been negatively responsive to information concerning the Holy Ghost and the gifts of the Spirit, including speaking in other tongues, should write the Biblical reference, "Titus 3:5," inside the cover of their Bible which says,

*"… according to his mercy he <u>**saved**</u> us, by (1) the washing of regeneration and (2) **renewing of the Holy Ghost.**"*

Being saved is a two-fold process. First the washing and cleansing by the blood of Jesus, and then the "new creature" renewing by the Holy Ghost. This is God's way of saving a repentant sinner. How could anyone discount the Holy Ghost from the salvation process? The Biblical fact is, the Holy Ghost is an indispensable spiritual agent in God's process of saving by his grace.

Justification and regeneration involves the operation of the Holy Ghost, who cannot be left out of the equation. He is a vital and irreplaceable link to Jesus and the Heavenly Father. Carefully read again Titus 3:5-7. It was clear in Peter's mind that one shall receive the Holy Ghost when they believe for, and receive salvation. Peter had this same belief which he stated on the day of Pentecost, **"ye shall receive."**

- *ACT 2:38 Then Peter said unto them, Repent, and be baptized every one of you in the name of Jesus Christ for the remission of sins, <u>and ye shall receive the gift of the Holy Ghost</u>.*
  39 For the promise is unto you, and to your children, and to all that are afar off, even as many as the Lord our God shall call.

These scriptures give no indication that a delay in receiving the Holy Ghost occurred. It was an automatic operation of grace in the experience of those who believe in Jesus Christ. Therefore one should accept by faith the fact that they have been baptized in the Holy Ghost. They should also expect by faith to see immediate evidence of the converted life and the empowered life, just as Jesus said:

- *ACT 1:8 But <u>ye shall receive power</u>, after that the Holy Ghost is come upon you: and ye shall be witnesses unto me both in Jerusalem, and in all Judaea, and in Samaria, and unto the uttermost part of the earth.*

The fruit of the Spirit should become evident as a result of the indwelling of the Spirit. The old sinful man is crucified with Christ and it becomes his spiritual nature to live a new life.

- *GAL 5:22 But the fruit of the Spirit is love, joy, peace, longsuffering, gentleness, goodness, faith,*
  23 Meekness, temperance: against such there is no law.
  24 And they that are Christ's have crucified the flesh with the affections and lusts.
  25 If we live in the Spirit, let us also walk in the Spirit.

All of the gifts of the Spirit, including speaking in tongues, should be expected and accepted by faith as potentially possible and probable as needed in the spiritual life and warfare of the believer. Not one single manifestation can be logically deleted, neglected, or omitted. Speaking in tongues as a means of worship and praying should be embraced and believed ... and accepted by faith.

- *1CO 12:7 But the manifestation of the Spirit is given <u>to every man</u> to profit withal.*
  8 For to one is given by the Spirit the word of wisdom; to another the word of knowledge by the same Spirit;
  9 To another faith by the same Spirit; to another the gifts of healing by the same Spirit;
  *10 To another the working of miracles; to another prophecy; to another discerning of spirits; **to another divers kinds of tongues**; to another the interpretation of tongues:*
  11 But all these worketh that one and the selfsame Spirit, dividing <u>to every man</u> severally as he will.
  12 For as the body is one, and hath many members, and all the members of that one body, being many, are one body: so also is Christ.
  13 For by one Spirit <u>are we all baptized</u> into one body, whether we be Jews or Gentiles, whether we be bond or free; and have been all made to drink into one Spirit.
  14 For the body is not one member, but many.

Every member in the body of Christ should expect to manifest the gifts of the Spirit as he directs. Read verse eleven again which says:

- *1CO 12:11 But all these worketh that one and the selfsame Spirit, <u>dividing to every man</u> severally as he will.*

Emphasis should here be placed on Speaking in other tongues because of its importance, and the primary reason its function is needed, and given by God. Emphasis should be placed on the word, *"Intercession."*

When one speaks in tongues two primary actions are taking place, which are **"worship of God,"** and **"intercession."**

When the Holy Spirit was given on the day of Pentecost, people from fifteen different nations heard the Christians speaking in tongues, who were speaking in the foreign languages of those nations. They were worshiping and praising God. The foreigners said,

- *ACT 2:11 ... we do hear them speak in our tongues the wonderful works of God.*

Intercession

Intercession is a ministry of the Holy Spirit which should be highly appreciated and desired by every Christian, and make everyone want the infilling of the Holy Spirit, especially because of the gift of praying in other tongues.

When a believer is praying in other tongues, there is always the possibility that the Holy Spirit is interceding with God on their behalf concerning their needs. When, because of our human limitations we do not know for what to pray, the Spirit can make intercession about needs which we would not be able to express in agonizing prayers.

The Holy Spirit lives within Christians twenty-four hours a day, and he know exactly what is needed, and he makes **intercession** for the saints according to the will of God.

- *ROM 8:26 Likewise the Spirit also helpeth our infirmities: for we know not what we should pray for as we ought: but the Spirit itself maketh **intercession** for us with groanings which cannot be uttered (which we could not utter).*

27 And he that searcheth the hearts knoweth what is the mind of the Spirit, __because he maketh intercession for the saints according to the will of God__.

He that searcheth the heart is God. When the Holy Ghost intercedes for the saints, God knows what is on the mind of the Spirit. Speaking in tongues is a spiritual gift which everyone should desire, because the Holy Spirit is speaking to God. This gives a reason why every follower of Christ should "desire" to pray in tongues, because the Holy Spirit may be making intercession with God on their behalf.

Prophecy

- *1CO 14:1 Follow after charity, and desire spiritual gifts, but rather that ye may prophesy.*
2 For he that speaketh in an unknown tongue speaketh not unto men, but unto God: for no man understandeth him; howbeit in the spirit he speaketh mysteries.
3 But he that prophesieth speaketh unto men to edification, and exhortation, and comfort.
4 He that speaketh in an unknown tongue edifieth himself; but he that prophesieth edifieth the church.

From this scripture we can know that prophesy is very important. When one speaks in tongues they are speaking to God, and not to men, therefore "no man understands them (V. 2). When one prophesies they are speaking by the anointed utterance of the Holy Spirit, but they are speaking in their own language, therefore men can understand them, and can benefit from that which the Spirit says, teaches, and instructs. Prophesy is listed as a gift of the Spirit.

Interpretation of Tongues

The importance of prophesy cannot be over-stated because it is extremely valuable in an assembled meeting of the church where truth is being declared by the Holy Spirit, and must be clearly understood.

- *1CO 14:5 I would that ye all spake with tongues but rather that ye prophesied: for greater is he that prophesieth than he that speaketh with tongues, **except he interpret**, that the church may receive edifying.*

Three audible spoken gifts of the Holy Ghost are explained in the scripture. They are as follows:

1. Speaking in other tongues
2. Interpretation of Tongues
3. Prophecy

They are all called supernatural gifts of the Holy Spirit, and each serves a unique function and purpose in spiritual worship. When speaking in tongues occurs in an assembled meeting of Christians, and the attention of the congregation is drawn to a maximum of three persons who separately speak in tongues. The Bible instructs that one person should interpret the messages by the Holy Ghost in the language of the congregation so they might understand what was said in tongues.

The following passage answers several important questions regarding spiritual worship which is being enjoyed today by an increasing number of congregations who are becoming familiar with Holy Ghost worship.

- *1CO 14:26 How is it then, brethren? when ye come together, every one of you hath a psalm, hath a doctrine, hath a tongue, hath a revelation, hath an interpretation. Let things be done unto edifying.*

  27 If any man speak in an unknown tongue, let it be by two, or at the most by three, and that by course; and let one interpret.

  28 But if there be no interpreter, let him keep silence in the church; and let him speak to himself, and to God.

  29 Let the prophets speak two or three, and let the other judge.

  30 If any thing be revealed to another that sitteth by, let the first hold his peace.

  31 For ye may all prophesy one by one, that all may learn, and all may be comforted.

  32 And the spirits of the prophets are subject to the prophets.

  33 For God is not the author of confusion, but of peace, as in all churches of the saints.

According to world-wide news reports, the fastest growing phase of Christianity involves church bodies of worshippers who are being converted by the millions into Bible believing saints who are embracing spiritual Holy Spirit worship such as described in the above passage of Scripture.

Every Christian must accept and believe the Bible to be the authoritative word of God. If so, one must not delete, ignore, omit, or change anything to suit their interpretations or desires. One must bury all prejudice and past traditions which reject the fullness of the Spirit, and accept the abiding of the Holy Spirit as resident in every born again child of God ... and walks in the truth that they received the Holy Spirit when they were born again. The scripture says the following:

- 1CO 12:7 *"But the manifestation of the Spirit **is given to every man** to profit withal."*

Since the day of Pentecost, the Holy Spirit has been given to each person who has been born again by receiving Christ into their heart.

Sad to say, many have not experienced the fullness of this truth for various reasons. Failure to live and walk in the Spirit has been a matter of ignorance, not knowing what the Bible says about the matter.

Another reason is, living among an environment which smothers or repels truth having to do with the Holy Spirit and speaking in tongues. Denominational indoctrination and prejudice stands in first position of opposition against any involvement pertaining to the Holy Spirit and speaking in tongues.

The author of this book desires to help people who have been saved, but who have little knowledge regarding the Holy Ghost. The author's motive is to show scripturally that when God saves an individual, He also gives them the gift of the Holy Ghost. The author also desires to Biblically show that the Holy Ghost can **speak to God** through them in languages (tongues) unknown to them. The Bible says very much about this.

- *1CO 14:2 For he that speaketh in an unknown tongue speaketh not unto men, but unto God: for no man understandeth him; howbeit in the spirit he speaketh mysteries.*
- *ACT 2:4 And they were all filled with the Holy Ghost, and began to speak with other tongues, as the Spirit gave them utterance.*
- *ROM 8:26 Likewise the Spirit also helpeth our infirmities: for we know not what we should pray for*

> *as we ought: but the Spirit itself maketh intercession for us with groanings which cannot be uttered.*
> *27 And <u>he that searcheth the hearts</u> knoweth what is the mind of the Spirit, because he maketh intercession for the saints according to the will of God.*

"He that searcheth the hearts" is God. Every person who has been saved by God's grace should <u>**earnestly contend**</u> to enjoy this same gift of faith concerning the Holy Ghost.

- *JUD 1:3 Beloved, when I gave all diligence to write unto you of the common salvation, it was needful for me to write unto you, and exhort you that ye should <u>earnestly contend</u> for the faith which was once delivered unto the saints.*

NOTE: An address for correspondence is given at the end of this book.

6

A Gift From God

Earnest

Based on the word of God, after a person is born again through believing in Christ, they are given the Holy Spirit as a promissory seal (earnest) of their eternal inheritance.

> • *EPH 1:13 In whom ye also trusted, after that ye heard the word of truth, the gospel of your salvation: in whom also **after that ye believed, ye were sealed with** that holy Spirit of promise,*
> *14 Which is the **earnest** of our inheritance until the redemption of the purchased possession, unto the praise of his glory.*

One must take this passage (Ephesians 1:13-14) as confirmation of a promise-pledge of a gift from God, that after one is born again God seals the spiritual transaction by giving the Holy Spirit as the **earnest** of his promise of eternal life. (Verse 14)

One should not underestimate the value of the **GIFT** of the Holy Spirit which God has given to every believer. The word **"earnest"** which is applied to the Holy Spirit has powerful and significant meaning.

The dictionary has several definitions and interpretations of the word "earnest," but there is one which definitely applies to the above scripture.

The Merram-Webster Dictionary defines "earnest" as

"a token of what is to come: a PLEDGE."

As I considered and prayed about the meaning of the word "earnest" I associated it with the word "interest," as involved with a financial business transaction. As I searched the word of God, I concentrated on the passage of scripture which contained the word "earnest."

When I prayerfully studied the scripture I began to sense that God was speaking to me through the Holy Ghost. It came to me that the word "earnest" in this passage had a specific meaning. I focused on the portion of the passage which says,"

"ye were sealed with that <u>holy Spirit which is the</u> "__earnest__" of our inheritance until the redemption of the purchased possession."

I saw that the word "__earnest__" was making reference to the Holy Spirit which is the earnest of our inheritance which was promised by the Father. I asked God to give me some way to explain this truth. The following was immediately placed into my mind as an example of a transaction where an "earnest" is a "Pledge."

"Let's suppose that a prosperous farmer, who is a father, gives the home place on his farm to his son. The home place is the residence in which the farm-owner lives. He then tells his son there is more to come. He explains that he has made out his will, and eventually the entire farm will be given to him.

"The home place was the first evidence of the promised

inheritance of the Son, which in a legal term would be called an **"earnest"** of the promise of the Father.

"When God, the Father gives the gift of the Holy Ghost to a believer, it is an "earnest" of that inheritance which is to come in the future. The gift of the home place was a seal of the deal, which is called in the dictionary, a token of what is to come … a PLEDGE … an "earnest." The scripture continues, **"until the redemption of the <u>purchased possession.</u>"**

What is the purchased possession? The "purchased possession" is every born again believer who has been purchased by the blood of Jesus, and will eventually be eternally redeemed.

- *ACT 20:28 Take heed therefore unto yourselves, and to all the flock, over the which the Holy Ghost hath made you overseers, to feed the church of God,* **which he hath purchased with his own blood.**
- *1CO 6:20 For ye are bought with a price: therefore glorify God in your body, and in your spirit, which are God's.*

I saw it! The **GIFT** of the Holy Ghost was a token gift, or a pledge of something even more and greater to come when the purchased possession is eternally redeemed and makes it to heaven.

The gift of the Holy Ghost is an **"earnest"** of the believer's **inheritance**. We have a **pledge** from God, which is his promise of eternal life in heaven, with streets of gold, a mansion in the Father's house, a river of life, gates of pearl, and living eternally with God the Father, his Son Jesus Christ, the Holy Spirit, an innumerable host of angels, and the Heavenly Jerusalem in a New Heaven and a New Earth.

Let's read again about the Holy Ghost as the **"earnest"** of our promised inheritance. Folks, the gift of the Holy Ghost is a pledge from God the Father that there is more to come!

- *EPH 1:13 In whom ye also trusted, after that ye heard the word of truth, the gospel of your salvation: in whom also after that ye believed, ye were sealed with that <u>holy Spirit</u> of promise,*
  14 Which is the earnest of our inheritance <u>until the redemption of the purchased possession</u>, unto the praise of his glory.

"Until the redemption" … Until we get to heaven where our inheritance is fully redeemed!!

Everyone who has been born again must be aware that they were given the gift of the Holy Ghost when they were saved. Because of this gift they can enjoy a Spirit-filled life with awareness that the Holy Spirit is the "earnest" of their eternal inheritance which is to come. And, until that inheritance is obtained, one should expect in this life to enjoy the fruits of the Spirit and gifts of the Spirit which accompany the indwelling of the Holy Spirit.

The Spirit of Christ

In the eighth chapter of Romans it is clear that the indwelling Holy Spirit was the Spirit that empowered Christ in his earthly ministry, and it is this same spirit which dwells within all Christians today. In fact, if one does not have this Spirit within them under these circumstances, then the clear summary is, they do not belong to Christ, meaning *"he is none of his."*

- *ROM 8:9 But ye are not in the flesh, but in the Spirit, if so be that the Spirit of God dwell in you. Now if any man have not the Spirit of Christ, <u>he is none of his</u>.*

The Holy Ghost was the Spirit which dwelled in Christ. The Holy Ghost was the *"Spirit of Christ"* which anointed him.

Christ came to earth in the form of an ordinary man, and was called "the Son of man." It was necessary for him to be filled with the Holy Spirit in order to fulfill his ministry. He was baptized with the Holy Spirit while standing in the Jordan River during John the Baptist's ministry. From that moment on he was led of the Spirit. Peter had this to say about the matter.

- *ACT 10:38 How God anointed Jesus of Nazareth with the Holy Ghost and with power: who went about doing good, healing all that were oppressed of the devil; for God was with him.*

It is in this context that the terms *"Spirit of Christ"* and *"Spirit of God"* are making reference to the abiding Holy Ghost personally within Christ, since he is the agent of the Godhead that administers the will of the Father and his Son in the earth. An important point to see in this is, *"if any man have not the Spirit of Christ, he is none of his."* This means that every person who belongs to Christ has received the abiding infilling of the Holy Ghost; otherwise they do not belong to Christ.

With this in mind, all Christian believers must be careful about saying they do not have the Holy Ghost. One must realize that if they are saved, they **do** have the Holy Ghost dwelling within them. He may be so ignorantly unrecognized, suppressed and quenched that his indwelling is not obvious, therefore this is why every believer must stir up the gift which is within them.

- *2TI 1:6 Wherefore I put thee in remembrance that thou stir up the gift of God, which is in thee...*

One must be aware of traditional religious beliefs that will deny anyone the right to receive the Holy Spirit if it does not agree with their prescribed doctrinal guidelines. One's prejudicial doctrines will exclude those who do not meet standards set by their peers. This includes the traditional Pentecostal requirement that one must speak in other tongues before they can claim to be a temple of the Holy Ghost.

Speaking in other tongues (languages) is a gift of the Holy Ghost, and must be accepted by faith based on the promise of God that he gives the Holy Ghost to everyone who is saved by his grace.

One must believe the gift of the Holy Spirit is the "**earnest**" of our promised eternal inheritance … recorded, and documented in the records of heaven. Because of this one should fully accept they have the potential for experiencing all the gifts of the Spirits, including speaking in other tongues by the utterance of the Holy Ghost.

The indwelling of the Holy Spirit should be accepted by faith as a fact, based on the promise that God gives the Holy Spirit to everyone who obeys him. One's claim to having the Holy Ghost must be based on a sincere belief that they have experienced the new birth. Anyone who has been saved can rest assured, based on the Bible, that the Holy Spirit abides within their body as his temple, and they have the full potential to experience the manifestation of any of the gifts of the Spirit, especially the gift of speaking in tongues, because this was manifested through all Christians on the day of Pentecost as a sign (**"earnest"**) from God that the Holy Spirit was abiding in them.

- *ACT 2:4 And they were **all** filled with the Holy Ghost, and began to speak with other tongues, as the Spirit gave them utterance.*

This assurance based on the word of God should be acknowledged and accepted even before one speaks in tongues.

- *1CO 6:19 What? know ye not that your body is the temple of the Holy Ghost which is in you, which ye have of God, and ye are not your own?*
20 For ye are bought with a price: therefore glorify God in your body, and in your spirit, which are God's.

We can know for sure that Jesus also abides within us because we have the indwelling of the Spirit. The gift of the Spirit is the knowing confirmation of salvation, because Jesus is the Baptizer..

- *1JO 3:24 And he that keepeth his commandments dwelleth in him, and he in him.* ***And hereby we know that he abideth in us, by the Spirit which he hath given us.***

A sincere believer should desire to experience supernatural manifestations of the indwelling Holy Spirit. Every member of the body of Christ must accept this by faith, and be willing to move on into the deeper things of the Spirit from the point of conversion. This includes all the manifestations and gifts of the Spirit ... including speaking in other tongues. No single gift should be omitted or considered unnecessary ... or forbidden. Paul covered all this in his advice and admonitions:

The Gift of Prophesy

- *1CO 14:1 Follow after charity, and desire spiritual gifts, but rather that ye may prophesy.*
1CO 14:39 Wherefore, brethren, covet to prophesy, and forbid not to speak with tongues.
40 Let all things be done decently and in order.

The manifestation of the gift of prophesy is where the Holy Spirit speaks through a believer using their native language, both of the speaker and the hearers. Let me say at this point that it is marvelous when the Holy Spirit speaks through a believer in the supernatural manifestation of a foreign language that is unknown to the speaker, and normally unknown to the hearers. But, it is equally marvelous when the Holy Spirit empowers a believer to supernaturally speak prophetically in their own native language. Prophesy is just as supernatural as speaking in other tongues.

- *1CO 14:3 But he that prophesieth speaketh unto men to edification, and exhortation, and comfort.*

Therefore, it is implied that the hearers understand what is said in their own language.

Spirit of God ... Spirit of Christ ... Holy Spirit ... Holy Ghost

The designation, *"Holy Ghost"* is found in the King James Version 89 times, while *"Holy Spirit"* is found 7 times. Other versions of the Bible use *"Holy Spirit"* exclusively.

To some people, *"Holy Spirit"* seems more refined, since the term *ghost* has often carried a spooky, Halloween type association. This is not the way with me, and I am hardly aware of which designation I use. The preponderance of my Bible study has been from the King James Version; therefore I use the designation *"Holy Ghost"* without being aware. The terms *"Holy Ghost"* and *"Holy Spirit"* are the same, just as are the terms *"ghost"* and *"spirit."*

Many become confused concerning the identity of the Spirit, thinking that, perhaps, he is not a distinct spiritual being, but just an extension of God, because, as mentioned above, he is sometimes called *"the Spirit of God,"* and sometimes, *"the Spirit of Christ."* Therefore, some conclude that the Holy Spirit is just a spiritual extension of God, but not a spiritual person who is distinctly separate from God or Christ. But, the truth is, the Holy Spirit is a distinct divine person, as so are the Father and the Son. Biblical identifiers of the Holy Ghost are the *"Holy Spirit,"* the *"Spirit,"* the *"Spirit of God,"* and the *"Spirit of Christ."*

The pronoun *"He"* is used many times, indicating the Holy Ghost exists as a distinct and definite person. This is because he is the Spiritual Person through which God and Jesus operate in the earth today. He is the administrator of God's will, and of Christ's will.

Before the birth of Jesus on earth, all three Divine Persons in the Godhead operated from the vantage point of heaven. When the Son of God came to earth, The Father and Holy Spirit remained in heaven. When Jesus ascended back to heaven, the Holy Spirit was sent to earth to dwell within the bodies of all Christians. The Father and the Son are presently in heaven, and the indwelling Holy Spirit on earth gets his directions and instructions from them. Jesus said the following,

- *JOH 16:13 (NIV) But when <u>he</u>, the Spirit of truth, comes, <u>he</u> will guide you into all truth. <u>He</u> will not speak on his own; <u>he</u> will speak only what <u>he</u> hears, and <u>he</u> will tell you what is yet to come.*
  14 <u>He</u> will bring glory to me by taking from what is mine and making it known to you.

The Spirit abides within the church by dwelling within each individual member that makes up the church. The Father and the Son are in constant communication with the Holy Spirit who dwells within each believer for twenty-four hours a day. The Spirit is always aware of their needs, and he makes intercession with God concerning those needs. The Holy Spirit is always in touch with the needs of those in whom he dwells.

- *ROM 8:26 (NIV) In the same way, the Spirit helps us in our weakness. We do not know what we ought to pray for, but <u>the Spirit himself</u> intercedes for us with groans that words cannot express.*
  27 And he who searches our hearts knows the mind of the Spirit, because the Spirit intercedes for the saints in accordance with God's will.

"He who searches our hearts" is God in heaven. He is watching over us and looking out for our best interest. The Holy Spirit which dwells within our body-temple is in constant communication with God on our behalf. The Spirit never asks amiss because he always asks in keeping with the will of God, *"because the Spirit intercedes for the saints in accordance with God's will"* (v. 27).

It is no wonder that Paul exclaimed in verse 31,*"if God be for us, who can be against us?"*

Resurrection life

The Holy Spirit brings about resurrection into a new way of life by taking up his abode in every newly converted believer. This is how the new birth comes about. Just as God, through his own Spirit raised Jesus from the dead, he now, through the Holy Spirit, raises the sinner unto newness of life.

- *ROM 8:11 But if the Spirit of him that raised up Jesus from the dead dwell in you, he that raised up Christ from the dead shall also <u>quicken</u> your mortal bodies by his Spirit that dwelleth in you.*

This is precisely when the Holy Spirit takes up his abode in a newly born again believer. The same Holy Spirit which indwelled

Christ (the Spirit of Christ) now dwells in all who are thus resurrected by his power, just as Jesus became alive again while laying in the grave.

- *ROM 6:5 For if we have been planted together in the likeness of his death, we shall be also in the likeness of his resurrection: 6 Knowing this, that <u>our old man</u> is crucified with him, that the body of sin might be destroyed, that henceforth we should not serve sin.*
  7 For he that is dead is freed from sin.
  8 Now if we be dead with Christ, we believe that we shall also live with him:

During the experience of regeneration, the sinful creature, called "the old man," must be crucified with Christ. A literal experience occurs wherein the sinful, lustful, hateful, works and desires of the flesh die and are buried as identification with Christ's baptism into death. At this point, the Holy Spirit is given as an inseparable part of the new birth process which is described as *"being born of the Spirit."* The Holy Spirit is given to everyone who becomes thus identified with Christ.

This sanctification by the Spirit prompts "thanks to God."

- *2TH 2:13 But we are bound to give thanks alway to God for you, brethren beloved of the Lord, because God hath from the beginning chosen you to salvation through sanctification of the Spirit and belief of the truth:*

Manifestation by the Spirit is given.

- *1CO 12:7 But the manifestation of the Spirit is given to every man to profit withal.*

Believers in Christ are *"sealed"* by the Spirit.

- *2CO 1:22 Who hath also sealed us, and given the earnest of the Spirit in our hearts.*

The Gift of the Spirit is an *"earnest," down payment, surety deposit,"* of that promised to come eternally.

- *2CO 5:5 Now he that hath wrought us for the selfsame thing is God, who also hath given unto us the earnest of the Spirit.*

The Gift of the Spirit is assurance that we dwell in Christ, and Christ dwells in us.

- *1JO 3:24 And he that keepeth his commandments dwelleth in him, and he in him. And hereby we know that he abideth in us, by the Spirit which he hath given us.*
- *1JO 4:13 Hereby know we that we dwell in him, and he in us, because he hath given us of his Spirit.*

Baptized into Christ

Scriptural references to "baptism into Christ" have been mistakenly applied to "water baptism". One must realize that the spiritual experience of <u>Baptism into Christ</u> is not the same as baptism in water. The term "baptism" means *to be placed into*. It is exactly what it says, a baptism "into" Christ ... which means the precise time when one is placed into Christ.

One must maintain a distinct understanding of "baptism into Christ" without thinking of water when reading such scriptures as the following:

- *ROM 6:3 Know ye not, that so many of us as were baptized into Jesus Christ were baptized into his death?*
- *4 Therefore we are buried with him by baptism into death: that like as Christ was raised up from the dead by the glory of the Father, even so we also should walk in newness of life.*

When these scriptures are taken to mean water baptism, serious doctrinal errors occur. By making water baptism the means by which one is saved, makes it essential to salvation. This mistaken interpretation means that one is saved by the blood ... plus water. This cannot be true because one is saved by the blood plus nothing.

"Baptized into Christ" simply means to be "placed into Christ." A close study of the rest of the above chapter will convince one that a spiritual baptism wherein one is placed into Christ is the issue, and not a physical experience of baptism in water.

Jesus used the statement, *"abide in me,"* which is also analogous to being placed into Christ. There are many scriptures which speak of being "in" Christ.

- *JOH 15:7 If ye abide in me, and my words abide in you, ye shall ask what ye will, and it shall be done unto you.*

Baptism into Christ brings about the new birth. In fact, water baptism is a symbolic act which depicts the baptism into Christ, and should occur only after one has been baptized into Christ. The rite of water baptism cannot bring about the new birth.

Only baptism into Christ can do that. The baptism into Christ is essential to salvation.

Understanding this enables one to distinguish between scriptures which are speaking concerning baptism in water and baptism into Christ. Both baptisms are scripturally authentic but are distinctly different. One is a physical action of the flesh and the other is a work of the Spirit in the heart.

The precise Moment

During the spiritual process of the new birth several things occur. The first occurs when one is spiritually crucified and buried with Christ. It is at this precise moment when the Holy Spirit comes in as a resurrection force ... bringing forth a new creature in Christ Jesus. This is why the Biblical terminology is used which says *"baptized with the Holy Ghost."*

John the Baptist said:

- *MAR 1:8 I indeed have baptized you with water: but he shall baptize you with the Holy Ghost.*

Jesus said:

- *ACT 1:5 For John truly baptized with water; but ye shall be baptized with the Holy Ghost not many days hence.*

Water baptism is symbolic of the death, burial, and resurrection of Christ. It is also symbolic of the spiritual death and resurrection of the carnal man which occurs when one is born again by being baptized with the Holy Spirit.

Being baptized with the Holy Ghost at the moment of obtaining salvation is a prerequisite for baptism in water. One is not baptized in water in order to be saved, but because they have been saved. Water baptism is an outward statement of an inner experience. It is a public statement of identification with Christ as one's Savior and Baptizer in the Holy Ghost. Notice how much the Spirit is involved in the process of the new birth.

- *ROM 8:9 But ye are not in the flesh, but in the Spirit, if so be that the Spirit of God dwell in you. Now if any man have not the Spirit of Christ, he is none of his.*
10 And if Christ be in you, the body is dead because of sin; but the Spirit is life because of righteousness.
11 But if the Spirit of him that raised up Jesus the dead dwell in you, he that raised up Christ from the dead shall also <u>quicken</u> your mortal bodies by his Spirit that dwelleth in you.

Dictionary Definition of "quicken"

<u>transitive verb</u>

1a: to make alive : REVIVE
b: to cause to be enlivened : STIMULATE

Romans 8:11 says, *"the Holy Spirit shall also quicken your mortal bodies by his Spirit that dwelleth in you."*
Because of this resurrection-life, we are no longer in bondage to sinful flesh, but can now live the Christian life through the "quickening" power of the Holy Spirit which makes it possible to overcome the flesh. Let's keep reading the above scripture:

- *12 Therefore, brethren, we are debtors, not to the flesh, to live after the flesh.*
  13 For if ye live after the flesh, ye shall die: but if ye through the Spirit do mortify the deeds of the body, ye shall live.

Baptized into his death

- *ROM 6:3 Know ye not, that so many of us as were **baptized into Jesus Christ** were baptized into his death?*

This is why Paul continues with the following statements which explain "baptism into Christ."

- *ROM 6:7 For he that is dead is freed from sin.*
  8 Now if we be dead with Christ, we believe that we shall also live with him:
  9 Knowing that Christ being raised from the dead dieth no more; death hath no more dominion over him.
  10 For in that he died, he died unto sin once: but in that he liveth, he liveth unto God.
  11 Likewise reckon ye also yourselves to be dead indeed unto sin, but alive unto God through Jesus Christ our Lord.
  12 Let not sin therefore reign in your mortal body, that ye should obey it in the lusts thereof.
  13 Neither yield ye your members as instruments of unrighteousness unto sin: but yield yourselves unto God, as those that are alive from the dead, and your members as instruments of righteousness unto God.

The above is totally descriptive of spiritual death with Christ, and resurrection-living *"unto God"* in the Holy Spirit, which includes all who have been born again, which Jesus called *"born of the Spirit*" (JOH 3:6,8). The possession of the Holy Spirit, and being led by him, is the factor which identifies the children of God. Biblically, the ones who can rightfully call God "Father" are those who possess the Holy Spirit. It is by the work of the Spirit that one is adopted into the Father's family.

- *ROM 8:14 For as many as are led by the Spirit of God, they are the sons of God.*
  15 For ye have not received the spirit of bondage again to fear; but ye have received the Spirit of adoption, whereby we cry, Abba, Father.

Notice that the *Spirit* of adoption uses a capital S, confirming that the Holy Spirit is the Divine Agent which administers the adoption into God's family. God, himself, has born witness to his adopted children that they are truly his children by giving them the Spirit.

- *16 The Spirit itself beareth witness with our spirit, that we are the children of God:*

How can one definitely know -- without any shadow of a doubt -- that they are saved? The Biblical answer is, "By knowing that God has given them the Holy Spirit."

- *1JO 3:24 And he that keepeth his commandments dwelleth in him, and he in him. **And hereby we know that he abideth in us, by the Spirit which he hath given us.***

Inseparable works of grace

Receiving the Holy Ghost is not a second, or third work of grace, but an *initial* work of grace, inseparable from the new birth. It is the incoming of the Holy Spirit into a person's being, his body, mind, soul, and spirit that brings about the birth of a new creature in Christ. It is the Spirit that quickeneth, making one alive in Christ.

One must realize the importance of Mary, the mother of Jesus, being overshadowed by the Holy Spirit.

- *MAT 1:20 But while he thought on these things, behold, the angel of the Lord appeared unto him in a dream, saying, Joseph, thou son of David, fear not to take unto thee Mary thy wife: for that which is conceived in her is of the Holy Ghost.*

It was the Holy Ghost that brought spontaneous new life into existence within Mary, which would provide the body in which Jesus would live and minister. This event demonstrates to the world the power of the Spirit to generate a new creature into existence within every believer.

- *2CO 5:17 Therefore if any man be in Christ, he is a new creature: old things are passed away;behold, all things are become new.*

Born of the flesh prior to Born of the Spirit

The birth of the new man (the new creature in Christ Jesus) is accomplished by a work of the Holy Spirit in the heart, mind, soul, and spirit of the old man (the unregenerate creature). Therefore, the close coordination between being saved and filled with the Holy Spirit is scripturally evident. Jesus made this clear to Nicodemus in the following statements. Jesus explained that a man must first be born of his mother (*"born of water"*) and then must be *"born of the Spirit."* Follow the sequence in these verses, while remembering that Jesus was answering Nicodemus' question regarding entering his mother's womb again and being born the second time:

- *JOH 3:5 Jesus answered, Verily, verily, I say unto thee, Except a man be **born of water** (human birth) **and of the Spirit**, he cannot enter into the kingdom of God.*
  *6 That which is **born of the flesh is flesh**; and that which is **born of the Spirit** is spirit.*
  *7 Marvel not that I said unto thee, **Ye must be born again**.*
  *8 The wind bloweth where it listeth, and thou hearest the sound thereof, but canst not tell whence it cometh, and whither it goeth: so is every one that is **born of the Spirit**.*

New birth evidence

Without doubt, the scriptural evidence of being filled with the Spirit is *the new life in Christ Jesus*. The sign that one has been baptized in the Spirit is the *new birth*. If one claims to have experienced the new birth, they should manifest the change this brings about by walking and living in the Spirit. There are multitudes of scriptures to support this.

The Holy Spirit does not come in after salvation has been accomplished and acquired, but salvation comes about because the Holy Spirit has come in, initiating the resurrection unto newness of life. Receiving the Holy Spirit is not a subsequent consequence, but is the initiator of the new birth experience. He comes into those who are ready to die with Christ, and then live with him.

- *ROM 6:5 For if we have been planted together in the likeness of his death, we shall be also in the likeness of his resurrection:*

> *6 Knowing this, that our old man is crucified with him, that the body of sin might be destroyed, that henceforth we should not serve sin.*
>
> *22 But now being made free from sin, and become servants to God, ye have your fruit unto holiness, and the end everlasting life.*

It has already been shown how this transformed life, and the continuing overcoming life is consequential to receiving the Holy Spirit. It is the same God that raised Jesus from the dead, and empowers the Holy Ghost to raise a sinner to newness of life while they are still in their mortal body.

- *ROM 8:11 But if the Spirit of him that raised up Jesus from the dead dwell in you, he that raised up Christ from the dead shall also quicken your mortal bodies by his Spirit that dwelleth in you.*

This is solid scriptural evidence that it is the Holy Spirit that enables one's mortal body to be quickened unto new life in Christ. This means in the here-and-now, while we are in these human bodies. This is why Jesus told the woman taken in adultery to *"go and sin no more"* (JOH 8:11).

Turning from the Law of Moses to Christ

There was great pressure on Jewish Christians to turn back to the law. Even though they had been convinced concerning the reality of Christ because of the amazing signs and wonders they had experienced, it was difficult for them to refrain from trying to mix law and grace. Converted Jews came under relentless pressure from their friends, relatives, and spiritual leaders because they no longer looked to the law of Moses for justification, but trusted Christ fully. The pressure would not be so relentless if those converted would just keep doing the religious ordinances and works of the law along with their new-found faith in Christ.

Paul knew that when one turns to Christ for justification and righteousness, they must cease from observing the law of Moses in any form. Paul is so emphatic that he calls them foolish for allowing anyone to persuade them to turn back to the works of the law.

These Jews had been filled with the Spirit because of their faith in Christ. Something so great had never happened to them when they were looking to the law. They had experienced great miracles, and this had not happened while they were under the law.

Because they had turned away from the Ordinances of the Law and had turned to keeping the commandments of Christ, they no longer observed the Mosaic commandments, such as sacrificing a lamb once each year, circumcision, Sabbath rules and laws, dietary laws against certain meats, observing Holy Days, associating with only Jews, and hundreds of religious Jewish laws of Moses.

When Jesus died on the cross approximately six hundred and thirteen Jewish Laws and ordinances were nailed to the cross with Christ, and were abolished.

- *EPH 2:15 Having **abolished** in his flesh the enmity, even **the law of commandments** contained in ordinances; for to make in himself of twain one new man, so making peace;*
  *16 And that he might reconcile both unto God in one body **by the cross**, having slain the enmity thereby:*

Today, instead of keeping the commandments of Moses, we keep the commandments of Christ. Jesus said,

- *JOH 14:15 If ye love me, keep my commandments.*

It is amazing that in the very next verse after making this statement, Jesus brought the Holy Ghost into the picture regarding the new Christian life-style.

- *JOH 14:16 And I will pray the Father, and he shall give you another Comforter, that he may abide with you for ever;*
  17 Even the Spirit of truth; whom the world cannot receive, because it seeth him not, neither knoweth him: but ye know him; for he dwelleth with you, and shall be in you.

Having begun in the Spirit

Then Paul makes an extremely significant statement which lets us know that receiving the Holy Spirit occurs at the very <u>beginning</u> of the salvation experience, and not as a second, or third work in a progressive process. Carefully and slowly read the following passage.

- *GAL 3:1 O foolish Galatians, who hath bewitched you, that ye should not obey the truth, before whose eyes Jesus Christ hath been evidently set forth, crucified among you?*
  2 This only would I learn of you, <u>Received ye the Spirit</u> by the works of the law, or by the hearing of faith?
  *3 Are ye so foolish? **<u>having begun in the Spirit</u>**, are ye now made perfect by the flesh?*
  5 ... He therefore that ministereth to you the Spirit, and worketh miracles among you, doeth he it by the works of the law, or by the hearing of faith?

Look closely at verse three: *"Are ye so foolish? having __begun__ in the Spirit, are ye now made perfect by the flesh* (doing the works of the law)*?"* This identifies the receiving of the Spirit as the *"beginning"* ... *"having begun in the Spirit."* This is the beginning point of salvation.

- *2TH 2:13 But we are bound to give thanks alway to God for you, brethren beloved of the Lord, because God hath <u>from the beginning</u> <u>chosen you to salvation through sanctification of the Spirit</u> and belief of the truth:*

One does not become a candidate for receiving the Holy Spirit because they got saved, but they got saved because sanctification by the Holy Spirit filled their heart, mind, soul, and spirit, in response to their belief of the truth about Jesus.

They believed they would stand before Jesus sometime to come, and they must presently obtain forgiveness from him for sins. They wanted to stand before him with those sins forgiven. They knew they must become a follower of Christ and serve him in his kingdom.

Christ is the judge of all these things, and when he is convinced concerning ones honesty and sincerity, he receives them as a disciple, forgives their sins, washes and cleanses their soul, spirit, heart and mind, and converts them into a new creature in Christ Jesus. Immediately, as confirmation of his grace and acceptance, he gives the Holy Ghost to spiritually and physically dwell within their body. This is the miracle of salvation, and explains what is meant by being "SAVED."

The beginning of the point of the new life in Christ is marked by the moment when one totally converts to Christ by faith in him, and empties their life and mind of everything else except Christ. This means sin, and all religion that is not centered in

Christ is washed away by the blood of Jesus. It is at this moment when God the Father and Jesus Christ cooperatively commission the Holy Spirit to take up occupancy, and move into the body temple of a person who has committed their allegiance to Christ through confession and repentance, and calling upon the Lord Jesus Christ.

- *ROM 10:13 For whosoever shall call upon the name of the Lord shall be saved.*

Oh, how desperately the entire church needs to hear this truth. It is sad to see hungry souls come forward for salvation and never be told the truth about the ministry which the Holy Spirit can do for them. It is through the Spirit that one is crucified with Christ, and is raised up through a new birth by the Holy Spirit, as Jesus told Nicodemus.

- *JOH 3:6 That which is born of the flesh is flesh; and that which is born of the Spirit is spirit.*
  7 Marvel not that I said unto thee, Ye must be born again.

This is how one becomes saved … born again … regenerated … washed.

- *TIT 3:5 Not by works of righteousness which we have done, but according to his mercy he saved us, by the washing of regeneration, **and renewing of the Holy Ghost;***

The salvation experience results from the renewing of the Holy Ghost.

- *ROM 8:13 … but if ye through the Spirit do mortify the deeds of the body, ye shall live.*

It is sad to see how the church is divided over the Baptism in the Holy Spirit – divided as Pentecostals and Non-Pentecostals. How wonderful it would be if all who believe in Christ could see and acknowledge, according to the scripture, that the process of salvation in every person is a work of the Holy Spirit who takes residence in each individual believer because of their faith in Christ.

The subsequent effect of this indwelling is that one is changed, born again, and becomes a new creature in Christ. A further effect is that the Holy Spirit brings the fruit of the Spirit with him and also the gifts of the Spirit. When a person is saved they have the potential for producing the fruit of the Spirit and manifesting all the gifts of the Spirit as they are needed. This brings spiritual growth and maturity as one learns to *"live in the Spirit ... and also walk in the Spirit."*

The Fruit of the Spirit

- *GAL 5:25 If we live in the Spirit, let us also walk in the Spirit*

This verse is preceded by a list of the fruits of the Spirit.

- *GAL 5:22 But the fruit of the Spirit is love, joy, peace, longsuffering, gentleness, goodness, faith,*
  23 Meekness, temperance: against such there is no law.
  24 And they that are Christ's have crucified the flesh with the affections and lusts.

The Christian life will manifest these fruits by the power of the Holy Spirit who abides in that person.

- *25 If we live in the Spirit, let us also walk in the Spirit.*

In addition to fruits of the Spirit, a list of Spiritual Gifts is also given in the Bible.

The Gifts of the Holy Spirit

- *1CO 12:7 But the manifestation of the Spirit is given to every man to profit withal.*

  8 For to one is given by the Spirit the word of wisdom; to another the word of knowledge by the same Spirit;

  9 To another faith by the same Spirit; to another the gifts of healing by the same Spirit;

  *10 To another the working of miracles; to another prophecy; to another discerning of spirits; to another <u>divers kinds of **tongues**</u>; to another the interpretation of tongues:*

  *11 **But all these <u>worketh</u> that one and the selfsame Spirit**, dividing <u>to every man</u> **severally** as he will.*

Severally

"Severally" means "individually," therefore, this truth regarding the gifts of the Spirit applies to every Christian *("each one")* individually.

One cannot conscientiously deduct "tongues" from this Biblical list of spiritual gifts, because it is included as one of the ways the Holy Spirit *"**<u>worketh</u>**" among men in the church. (Verse 11)*

7

The Times of Refreshing Shall Come

At this point a major question must be discussed. What about those who say they received the Holy Ghost **after** they were saved ... maybe a week, or month, or long after, even years later?

The question is fully answered by many New Testament scriptures which declares that everyone who comes to Christ for salvation always receive the gift of the Holy Ghost as a part of the salvation process at the same time when they are converted ... rather than "after."?

In light of what the Bible says, the answer is simple. The Holy Spirit is given at the time when one is born again, which Jesus called *"born of the Spirit."* This indicates that the Holy Spirit is even involved in the new birth process ... *"born of the Spirit."*

Many who have received the baptism in the Holy Ghost believe one does not receive the Holy Ghost when they are saved, but they believe the baptism in the Spirit is obtained as a separate experience. They believe this baptism in the Holy Ghost can occur when they are saved, or it can happen after they are saved, perhaps soon after, or possibly long after.

But, contrary to this, it will be shown by the Bible which clearly teaches that when one is saved, they are also given the Holy Spirit at that time as a part of the conversion process.

Manifestations of the gifts of the Spirit can immediately accompany the arrival and entrance of the Spirit, including speaking in other tongues, or may be manifested soon thereafter. The point is, God **does** give the gift of the Spirit at the moment when one is born of the Spirit.

The Holy Ghost is an indwelling Power from God. Jesus said the following:

- *ACT 1:8 But ye shall receive power, after that the Holy Ghost is come upon you ...*

It will be thoroughly shown by the scripture that **receiving the gift of the Holy Spirit is an important part of the salvation process**, and that every person who becomes a born again believer in Christ is, **at that time** given the Holy Ghost as an indwelling Spirit in their body which becomes a temple, or dwelling place of the Holy Ghost.

- *1CO 6:19 What? know ye not that your body is the temple of the Holy Ghost which is in you, which ye have of God, and ye are not your own?*
- *20 For ye are bought with a price: therefore glorify God in your body, and in your spirit, which are God's.*

The Times of Refreshing

The Prophet Isaiah was given a fore view of the time when the gift of the Holy Ghost would be poured out upon the Church.

- *ISA 28:11 For with stammering lips and another tongue will he speak to this people.*
  *12 To whom he said, This is the rest wherewith ye may cause the weary to rest; and **this is the refreshing:***

Peter knew this passage was beginning to be fulfilled on the day of Pentecost. Peter applied the word **"refreshing,"** taking it from the words of Isaiah. Peter knew this outpouring of the Holy Ghost, which included stammering lips and speaking in another tongue came from the prophesy of Isaiah, who said, "**this is the refreshing**."

Therefore, Peter declared, *"the times of **refreshing** shall come from the presence of the Lord,"* and that time had come! The manifesting of stammering lips and other tongues constituted the *times of "refreshing"* described by Isaiah.

The Holy Spirit is definitely this **refreshing**, which can Biblically refer only to the ministry of the Holy Ghost. Isaiah declared *"this is the refreshing."*

Repentance and **conversion**, and **sins blotted out**, are Biblically required before the Holy Ghost can come into a Christian believer as *"the Refreshing."*

- *ACT 3:19 **Repent** ye therefore, and be **converted**, that your **sins** may be **blotted out**, **when the times of refreshing "shall come" from the presence of the Lord.***

This confirms that the Holy Ghost is given by the Lord when one is saved . . . at the time of repentance and conversion.

When the Holy Ghost was newly rediscovered near the turn of the twentieth century, at that time every Christian believed they were already saved. Therefore, when they were confronted with news about the Holy Ghost, they received it as an experience which was additional to the experience of obtaining salvation.

Before that time, and going back for many centuries, very little was understood about the Holy Ghost because it had not been emphasized. In fact information about the Holy Spirit had been suppressed.

The opinion prevailed that receiving the Holy Ghost was a second, or an additional spiritual experience after obtaining salvation. This was because information about the Holy Ghost had not been openly considered for centuries.

Every Christian claimed to be saved, but had little or no knowledge regarding the Holy Ghost. When this truth was discovered to exist in the Bible, and God began to manifest the reality of the gift to the church at the beginning of the twentieth century, the baptism with the Holy Ghost should have been received as a key truth which God considered to be a part of the plan of salvation that had been missed for centuries.

Rather than believing the Holy Ghost was a key ingredient of God's overall plan of salvation, it was accepted to be a second spiritual experience in addition to being saved.

Information about the Holy Spirit had been in the word of God for over two thousand years, but truth about the Holy Ghost was smothered by Catholicism which decreed that only Catholic Priests could receive the indwelling of the Holy Spirit. Therefore a general knowledge about the Holy Ghost was not known or understood by the church.

This was further complicated by the fact that the only available Bible was written in Latin, and only Priests were educated to read it. Therefore the mass of churchmen were dependent upon Priests to read and interpret it to them.

Since the Catholic church dominated all facets of the institutional church for over one thousand years, during a period called the "dark ages," truth concerning the baptism in the Holy Spirit was totally silenced for many centuries.

But God uncovered this hidden truth by a mighty Holy Ghost revival, beginning with the Azusa Street church revival. The reason the impact of this revival was so earth shaking was because speaking with other tongues, just like that which had occurred on the day of Pentecost was emphasized.

When the great Holy Spirit outpouring occurred, receiving the Holy Ghost was held to be in addition to, and separate from being saved, and was considered a separate experience.

Even though there is a lack of Biblical support for this theory or doctrine, It has been believed since that time by almost everyone who has embraced receiving the Holy Ghost.

One must accept by faith what the word of God says, and must be willing to improve their believing by accepting the word of God over tradition. This requires believing by faith that the Holy Ghost is given by God in response to faith in Jesus. That kind of faith accepts Jesus as the Son of God, repents and believes in him to forgive sins, accepts him as the Lord of their life, and are <u>converted</u> to being a child of God. It is clear that at that moment God saves them by his grace, and gives the Holy Ghost to dwell within them.

Believing the doctrines and teachings of Christ is vitally important, especially concerning the Holy Ghost. Jesus was introduced by John the Baptist as the one who would baptize with the Holy Ghost.

When Jesus breathed upon his disciples and said, *"receive ye the Holy Ghost,"* he was anticipating their initial baptism which would come on the day of Pentecost. The disciples did not receive the Holy Ghost at the time Jesus breathed on them, because he clearly told them they would receive him *"not many days hence."* They were instructed to wait in Jerusalem until the Holy Ghost came upon them.

The promised Holy Ghost came to the church on the day of Pentecost, and Peter said the promise would continue to be available to everyone forever.

One must not reject the truth concerning the Holy Ghost, but should receive it with an open mind and an open heart. Receiving the Holy Ghost begins with spiritual acceptance of what Jesus and the Bible says about him.

When one *"receives"* and acknowledges the Holy Ghost, they accept and treat him like a dear friend or relative who is welcomed into their home, given the guest room and encouraged to stay as long as he likes, meaning indefinitely and permanently. Excitement fills the air over his presence. No extra effort is too much for such a wonderful guest.

The Holy Ghost abides within those who are saved because of their faith in Christ and his word. The Bible says their bodies become the dwelling place, or temple of the Holy Ghost.

- *1JO 2:27 But the anointing which ye have received of him abideth in you, and ye need not that any man teach you: but as the same anointing teacheth you of all things, and is truth, and is no lie, and even as it hath taught you, ye shall abide in him.*

One baptism -- Many fillings

There is an initial baptism, or "receiving" of the Holy Ghost, and many fillings thereafter. Regarding the Holy Spirit, Jesus told the woman at the well about the coming time when true worshipers would worship the Father in Spirit and in truth:

- *JOH 4:14 But whosoever drinketh of the water that I shall give him shall never thirst; but the water that I shall give him shall be in him a well of water springing up into everlasting life.*
  *23 ... **But the hour cometh, and now is, when the true worshippers shall worship the Father in spirit and in truth: for the Father seeketh such to worship him.***
  24 God is a Spirit: and they that worship him must worship him in spirit and in truth.

This time of worshipping in the Spirit began on the day of Pentecost, and has continued thereafter. Why not worship God in the Spirit, just as described by Jesus? The Spirit is exactly as Jesus said when he cried out to the spiritually thirsty Jews at the feast:

- *JOH 7:37 In the last day, that great day of the feast, Jesus stood and cried, saying, If any man thirst, let him come unto me, and drink.*
  38 <u>He that believeth on me</u>, as the scripture hath said, out of his belly shall flow rivers of living water.
  39 (But this spake he of the Spirit, <u>which</u> <u>they that believe on him should receive</u>: for the Holy Ghost was not yet given; because that Jesus was not yet glorified.)

From the scriptures we can deduct that the Holy Spirit is given to a person when they become a converted believer in Jesus. Therefore, the believing process of obtaining salvation includes receiving the gift of the Holy Ghost. In the above passage Jesus said concerning the Holy Ghost, "*which they that believe on him should receive:*"

From this we can say the Holy Ghost is given to those who become a true believer ... in fact he said those "that believe on him **should receive** the Holy Ghost (V. 39).

When one draws the water down to a low level in a well, it soon fills back up, because there is a running stream, or spring in the bottom of the well which keeps replenishing the supply. A flowing river is the same way. Jesus used a springing well, and a flowing river to illustrate the refreshing nature of the Holy Spirit.

After Peter was filled with the Holy Ghost occasions came for him to stand and preach concerning what had happened to them, and to magnify Christ as the crucified and risen Lord. Peter was unable to stand for Jesus prior to being filled with the Spirit, but instead, denied him. He became a different person after being filled with the Spirit, and was able to stand boldly before those same people. Special fillings for special occasions were given, such as when a crippled man was healed at the gate of the Temple:

- *ACT 4:8 Then Peter, <u>filled with the Holy Ghost</u>, said unto them, Ye rulers of the people, and elders of Israel,*
  9 If we this day be examined of the good deed done to the impotent man, by what means he is made whole;
  10 Be it known unto you all, and to all the people of Israel, that by the name of Jesus Christ of Nazareth, whom ye crucified, whom God raised from the dead, even by him doth this man stand here before you whole.

Now, do not miss this important point. Peter was filled with the Holy Ghost in the second chapter of Acts. Now, here in the fourth chapter he is said to be again *"filled with the Holy Ghost"* (v. 8).

Peter had the boldness to accuse them of crucifying Jesus, and to also declare that God had raised him from the dead. Peter was no longer bound by fear. This is one of the important functions of the Holy Ghost. He is the force behind spiritual power, and of love, and of a sound mind.

- *2TI 1:7 For God hath not given us the spirit of fear; but (the Spirit) of power, and of love, and of a sound mind.*

Peter made it clear that receiving the Holy Spirit was not just a one-time filling, but there would be many refillings and refreshings that would follow.

- *ACT 3:19 Repent ye therefore, and be converted, that your sins may be blotted out, <u>**when the times of refreshing shall come from the presence of the Lord.**</u>*

Peter was definitely making reference to the refilling of the Holy Ghost -- one baptism ... many fillings ... *"the <u>times</u> of refreshing shall come."* Peter was making reference to a prophesy of Isaiah concerning the Holy Ghost.

- *ISA 28:11 For with stammering lips and another tongue will he speak to this people.*
  12 To whom he said, This is the rest wherewith ye may cause the weary to rest; and <u>this is the refreshing</u>:

This refreshing had to do specifically with receiving the Holy Ghost into one's life. Peter's use of the word *"when"* means *at which time.* Notice (in Acts 3:19 above) the sequence of events involved, which occur in conjunction with the coming of this time of refreshing which comes from the presence of the Lord: (1) Repent; (2) Be converted; (3) Sins blotted out. These things happen in conjunction with, or at the time (4) one receives the initial refreshing from the presence of the Lord ... that refreshing being the baptism with the Holy Ghost.

The Comforter

A short time after the Holy Ghost was given on the day of Pentecost, the disciples were sorely persecuted by the Jewish religious leaders. They were put in jail, brought before the council, severely threatened, and commanded not to speak at all, nor teach in the name of Jesus (ACT 4:17-18). When they were released they *"went to their own company, and reported all that the chief priests and elders had said unto them."*

Jesus had said that the Holy Ghost would be the "comforter."

- *JOH 14:16 And I will pray the Father, and he shall give you another Comforter, that he may abide with you for ever;*
- *JOH 14:26 But the Comforter, which is the Holy Ghost, whom the Father will send in my name, he shall teach you all things, and bring all things to your remembrance, whatsoever I have said unto you.*

A wonderful example of the comforting of the Holy Ghost was experienced by the disciples after they left the Jewish council. The disciples had a right to be discouraged and spiritually drained, but instead, the well of the Spirit began to spring up until it became a flowing river. Instead of complaining, they began to pray one of the most outstanding prayers in the Bible. Without a doubt, the Holy Ghost made intercession for them with prayers they could not have uttered by themselves.

- *ACT 4:29 And now, Lord, behold their threatenings: and grant unto thy servants, that with all boldness they may speak thy word,*
  30 By stretching forth thine hand to heal; and that signs and wonders may be done by the name of thy holy child Jesus.

The disciples were praying for the exact opposite of what they had been commanded to do by the Jewish Council. They prayed, *"grant unto thy servants, that with all boldness they may speak thy word."* Notice what happened in the next verse. The refreshing came ... the re-filling came.

- *31 And when they had prayed, the place was shaken where they were assembled together; and they were all filled with the Holy Ghost, and they spake the word of God with boldness.*

These believers had already been filled with the Holy Ghost just a few days earlier, and yet, here it says, *"they were all filled with the Holy Ghost."* Isaiah had prophesied concerning the New Testament church -- who would speak with stammering lips and another tongue -- saying:

- *ISA 28:12 To whom he said, This is the rest wherewith ye may cause the weary to rest; and this is the refreshing:*

My Cup Runneth Over

The disciples did not suffer spiritual thirst ... the well was flowing ... they were refreshed by the Spirit -- the essence of what Jesus taught when he used a well ... and then a river ... to describe the refilling of the Spirit. There is an inexhaustible supply of spiritual power available to the believer through the Holy Ghost.

It is obvious that the disciples had already been filled with the Holy Ghost, and he was resident within each of them, therefore the subsequent statement, *"they were all filled with the Holy Ghost,"* indicates that the anointing of the Spirit will rise up at times of need for special ministry, spiritual warfare, operation of the gifts of the Spirit, or for comfort and peace during times of stress, duress, trouble and turmoil.

One can think of it in terms of renewing, or replenishing the supply. One's spiritual cup is filled and refilled continually. This is making reference to the repeated overflowing manifestations of the Spirit which will follow as needed for special anointing to minister and to utilize the gifts of the Spirit. This is how our inner man is renewed day by day (2CO 4:16). This is why Jesus told the Samaritan woman at the well that those who drink of the water that he gives will never thirst, meaning they will always have an abundant supply.

- *JOH 4:14 But whosoever drinketh of the water that I shall give him shall never thirst; but the water that I shall give him shall be in him a well of water springing up into everlasting life.*

David used oil to describe the way God keeps filling and refilling one's cup. Oil typified the Holy Spirit in the Old Testament. This is what David meant when he wrote the following:

- *PSA 23:5 Thou preparest a table before me in the presence of mine enemies: thou anointest my head with oil; my cup runneth over.*

This is what happened to the disciples. They were *"filled with the Holy Ghost"* again and again. The prophetic word concerning the Holy Ghost had become a reality in the lives of the believers who were going through *"the valley of the shadow of death."*

Jesus had told his disciples they would be given special power to be witnesses for him after the Holy Ghost had come upon them.

- *ACT 1:8 But ye shall receive power, after that the Holy Ghost is come upon you: and ye shall be witnesses unto me both in*

Jerusalem, and in all Judaea, and in Samaria, and unto the uttermost part of the earth.

The anointing

Anointing with oil was practiced in the Old Testament, and, as previously stated, was symbolic of the anointing of the Holy Spirit which would come to the New Testament church through the ministry of Christ. For today Jesus, himself, was the first to be anointed with the Holy Ghost on a continual, indwelling basis, just as would happen to those who make up the church.

- *ACT 10:38 How God anointed Jesus of Nazareth with the Holy Ghost and with power: who went about doing good, and healing all that were oppressed of the devil; for God was with him.*

The Pharisees were perplexed concerning John the Baptist, who he was, and from where had he come? They asked if he was a reincarnation of one of the great prophets ... or even the Christ ... which he denied. When they pinned him down with questions about himself, he presented himself as the introducer of the one who would baptize with the Holy Ghost.

- *JOH 1:24 And they which were sent were of the Pharisees.*
  25 And they asked him, and said unto him, Why baptizest thou then, if thou be not that Christ, nor Elias, neither that prophet?
  26 John answered them, saying, I baptize with water: but there standeth one among you, whom ye know not;
  27 He it is, who coming after me is preferred before me, whose shoe's latchet I am not worthy to unloose.

33 ... And I knew him not: but he that sent me to baptize with water, the same said unto me, Upon whom thou shalt see the Spirit descending, and remaining on him, the same is he which baptizeth with the Holy Ghost.

One of God's major objectives in sending his Son was that he might baptize believers with the Holy Ghost.

8

The Seal of Sonship

When the Son of God came to be manifested in human flesh he became a human in every respect and was also called *"the Son of man."* God ordained John the Baptist as the one who would introduce his Son. How was John to know exactly who this Son was? God gave John a sure sign. He showed him that after he baptized the Son of God in water, the Holy Spirit would descend in the form of a dove and remain on him. God confirmed his Son to John the Baptist, and to the rest of the world, by baptizing him with the Holy Spirit.

- *JOH 1:32 And John bare record, saying, I saw the Spirit descending from heaven like a dove, and it abode upon him. 33 And I knew him not: but he that sent me to baptize with water, the same said unto me, Upon whom thou shalt see the Spirit descending, and remaining on him, the same is he which baptizeth with the Holy Ghost. 34 And I saw, and bare record that **this is the Son of God**.*

Keep in mind that Jesus is our pattern and example in all things.

- *1PE 2:21 For even hereunto were ye called: because Christ also suffered for us, **leaving us an example, that ye should follow his steps:***

According to the New Testament plan of salvation, those who become sons of God are confirmed in the same way as was Jesus, by the gift of the Holy Spirit as a sign and seal of God's confirmation of sonship. The gift of the Holy Spirit serves as God's official seal of proof for all whom he adopts into sonship, and serves as confirmation of acceptance into his family. The gift of the Holy Spirit is proof that one has been born again. It proves one is a son of God. The Holy Spirit is the proof of adoption into the family of God, which gives one the right to call God their Father.

- *ROM 8:14 For as many as are led by the Spirit of God, they are the sons of God.*
  15 For ye have not received the spirit of bondage again to fear; but ye have received the Spirit of adoption, whereby we cry, Abba, Father.
  16 The Spirit itself beareth witness with our spirit, that we are the children of God:

Peter was called before a Jewish Council in Jerusalem because he had gone into the home of Cornelius, who was a Gentile. This was forbidden by Jews. Peter told the Council how God had called him by a vision to go preach to Gentiles. He told the Council how, while he was preaching, the Holy Ghost fell on every Gentile that was in the room.

Peter concluded the gift of the Holy Ghost is confirmation from God that repentance has been accepted, and forgiveness has been granted, and born again life has been issued to a new believer.

- *ACT 11:16 Then remembered I the word of the Lord, how that he said, John indeed baptized with water; but ye shall be baptized with the Holy Ghost.*
  17 Forasmuch then as <u>God gave them the like gift</u> as he did unto us, who believed on the Lord Jesus Christ; what was I, that I could withstand God?
  18 When they heard these things, they held their peace, and glorified God, saying, <u>Then hath God</u> to the Gentiles granted <u>repentance unto life.</u>

SUMMARY: When one receives the Holy Ghost, they can rest assured that this gift from God is proof and confirmation that God has forgiven their sins, and their repentance has been accepted with God.

- *ACT 15:8 And God, which knoweth the hearts, bare them witness, giving them the Holy Ghost, even as he did unto us;*

The Holy Spirit is the seal of approval which God gives to everyone after they believe in Christ. It is like a king's official seal stamped on a document, bearing witness to his official approval.

Believing is the Starting Point

The key ingredient for obtaining God's blessing is "believing." As God observes our effort to secure his help and provision, he looks into our attempts of faith. The spiritual element for which God most diligently searches to find is our "believing."

He requires that we believe in Him. He also demands that we believe in his Son, Jesus Christ. He requires that we believe in the Holy Ghost as the third divine person in the Godhead Trinity.

He expects that we believe the authenticity of his word.

Believing the Gospel of Christ is absolutely required. It would take much time and manuscript space to cover all aspects of "Believing,"

But, to get to the point concerning obtaining salvation, the basic requirement of God is "believing."

When God is convinced concerning one's believing in his Son, and believes in his word, that God responds to that believing, which prompts him to move forward in the process of regeneration, acknowledging confession, accepting repentance, giving forgiveness for sin, and giving the gift of the abiding Holy Ghost.

This is all a part of the overall process of salvation which transpires "after one believes." Carefully notice the words in the following verse, "after that ye believed."

- *EPH 1:13 In whom ye also trusted, after that ye heard the word of truth, the gospel of your salvation: <u>in whom also "after that ye believed," ye were sealed with that holy Spirit of promise,</u>*

Immediately after Believing

The last half of the above verse (which I have underlined) says it clearly. This confirms that one is sealed with the Holy Spirit as the fulfillment of God's promise to those who believe in Jesus. This scripture tells us that the gift of the Holy Ghost is God's response to those who believe ... "after" they believe.

When Peter reported to the brethren at Jerusalem regarding those believers at Cornelius' house who were baptized with the Holy Ghost, he identified them as those *"who believed on the Lord Jesus Christ."*

- *ACT 11:17 Forasmuch then as God gave them the like gift as he did unto us, <u>who believed on the Lord Jesus Christ</u>; what was I, that I could withstand God?*

There is no reason to believe there will be any delay in receiving this confirmation from God ... or that it might not happen expeditiously to those who believe on the Lord Jesus Christ.

An interesting song which used to be popular compared the human body to "This Old House." Picture in your mind three people walking over an old home-place. They come upon an old house that once knew life and occupancy. They determine to make it livable again, and to move into it themselves. They renew it, inside and out, repairing, painting, scrubbing and cleaning. By a cooperative effort they prepare it for residency and soon move in. Each one has done their part, and the goal is accomplished.

This is how regeneration is accomplished in the life of one who has been separated from God through the sin of Adam, and through their own sinfulness. All of the works of grace are accomplished in their body, mind, soul, and spirit. This work has all been accomplished by the **Father**, the **Son**, and the **Holy Spirit**. All three should be entitled to full right of occupancy, and each one should be received and appreciated for their unique role in the redemptive process. There should be no reason for any delay in the moving of each one of the three ... including the Holy Spirit. Immediate occupancy upon completion of redemption is the divine plan.

If there is any delay in recognizing, or accepting the reality of the Holy Spirit, it does not make him any less real or any less an occupant.

Receiving while denying certain gifts

The Non-Pentecostal position has been that one does receive the Holy Spirit when they are born again. And yet, they deny most of the manifestations of the gifts that scripturally confirm the presence and existence of the Holy Spirit in one's life and in the church.

But, the Holy Spirit is very real and dwells in the body-temple of everyone who is saved, even when the Spirit is not given the recognition he deserves. The truth that one receives the Holy Ghost immediately upon receiving salvation is described and explained by both John the Baptist and Jesus in the following two scriptures:

John the Baptist said,
Receiving the Holy Spirit follows repentance, which God requires:

- *MAT 3:11 I indeed baptize you with water unto **repentance**: but he that cometh after me is mightier than I, whose shoes I am not worthy to bear: he shall baptize you with the Holy Ghost, and with fire:*

Jesus said,
The Holy Spirit comes within to dwell after one becomes a true believer:

- *JOH 7:38 He that believeth on me, as the scripture hath said, out of his belly shall flow rivers of living water. (But this spake he of the Spirit, which they that believe on him should receive ...)*

One receives the Holy Ghost when they are placed (baptized) into Christ.

- *ACT 2:38 Then Peter said unto them, Repent, and be baptized every one of you in the name of Jesus Christ for the remission of sins, and ye shall receive the gift of the Holy Ghost.*

Obeying Christ is required for receiving the Holy Ghost.

- *ACT 5:32 And we are his witnesses of these things; and so is also the Holy Ghost, whom God hath given to them that obey him.*

The Holy Ghost is given to those who sincerely believe on the Lord Jesus Christ.

- *ACT 11:17 Forasmuch then as God gave them the like gift as he did unto us, who believed on the Lord Jesus Christ; what was I, that I could withstand God?*
  18 When they heard these things, they held their peace, and glorified God, saying, Then hath God also to the Gentiles granted repentance unto life.

God gives the Holy Ghost to those who truly believe the gospel.

- *ACT 15:7 … Peter rose up, and said unto them, Men and brethren, ye know how that a good while ago God made choice among us, that the Gentiles by my mouth should hear the word of the gospel, and **believe**.*
  8 And God, which knoweth the hearts, bare them witness, giving them the Holy Ghost, even as he did unto us;
  9 And put no difference between us and them, purifying their hearts by faith.

**Being sanctified by the Holy Ghost
makes one acceptable to God.**

- *ROM 15:16 That I should be the minister of Jesus Christ to the Gentiles, ministering the gospel of God, that the offering up of the Gentiles might be acceptable, being sanctified by the Holy Ghost.*

**A believer's body becomes the dwelling
place of the Holy Ghost.**

- *1CO 6:19 What? know ye not that your body is the temple of the Holy Ghost which is in you, which ye have of God, and ye are not your own?*

Regeneration and renewing is a work of the Holy Ghost.

- *TIT 3:5 Not by works of righteousness which we have done, but according to his mercy he saved us, by the washing of regeneration, and renewing of the Holy Ghost;*

**Possessing the Holy Ghost is a witness
of sanctification before God.**

- *HEB 10:14 For by one offering he hath perfected for ever them that are sanctified.*
  15 Whereof the Holy Ghost also is a witness to us:

All these scriptures unite to confirm that God is fully aware of all believers, and values their faith when they believe in his Son, Jesus Christ.

- *JOH 3:16 For God so loved the world, that he gave his only begotten Son, that **whosoever believeth in him** should not perish, but have everlasting life.*

God is anxious to give the Holy Ghost to everyone whom he judges to have sincerely and truly believed and repented. God's word says they are baptized into Christ, which means they have "put on Christ."

- *GAL 3:27 For as many of you as have been baptized into Christ have put on Christ.*
- *ACT 2:38 Then Peter said unto them, Repent, and be baptized every one of you in the name of Jesus Christ for the remission of sins, and ye shall receive the gift of the Holy Ghost.*

I suggest to anyone who has repented and believes God has forgiven their sins, and has saved them, **they should believe that when they were saved God gave them the gift of the Holy Ghost.** They should begin thanking God daily for his gift, and believing God's word, and expecting to experience Biblical confirmation by manifestations of the gifts of the Spirit, especially speaking in other tongues as the Spirit gives the utterance.

Uninformed and unaware

An actual lack of awareness exists on the part of those who are uninformed concerning the Holy Spirit. Without doubt, many local churches have been subjected to misinformed ministries, or denominational creeds which have not given the credulity to the Holy Spirit that he deserves. Of the three in the Godhead, the Holy Spirit has been most rejected and neglected theologically, while he is actually the representative of the Trinity which has been assigned earthly duty, and who dwells within the bodies of all converted believers. Satan has done a good job of keeping many sincere people uninformed and unaware concerning the reality of the Holy Spirit, and his indwelling presence within their bodies.

- *1CO 6:19 What?* **know ye not that your body is the temple of the Holy Ghost which is in you, which ye have of God,** *and ye are not your own?*
  20 For ye are bought with a price: therefore glorify God in your body, and in your spirit, which are God's.

A positive belief

My father, Rodney Oliver Symes, Sr., was operating a large ranch is central Colorado. Several people who had experienced the manifestation of the gifts of the Holy Ghost were supernaturally led to his house. None had known the others were coming, and, in fact, were not even acquainted.

The day was devoted to Bible study about the Holy Ghost, of which my father knew practically nothing. At the end of the day, dad and one of his hired hands went out to feed the hogs. Dad said to the other man, "Well, what do you think about all of this business concerning the Holy Ghost"?

The hired hand replied, "Well I don't know," and began to express his reservations. Dad responded, "<u>Well, I believe it</u>," and when he did, he felt a surge of supernatural emotional force go through him, and he knew the issue was settled with him. He had chosen to believe, and God had acknowledged that. He knew the Holy Ghost was God's gift to him and he wanted to experience the manifestations of his indwelling.

Needless to say, Dad received the manifestations and fullness of the Spirit a short time later, and the hired hand did not. This is the reason I said a few paragraphs back that "believing is the starting point."

When light becomes darkness

It is so easy to take a stand against truth. At that point, if Dad had taken the other direction, he probably would have never walked in the truth. Many have done this unwittingly, just falling in line with tradition, or their environment, heritage and background. Once they do this, they become an opponent of the truth, which is a terrible position in which to be, especially if one is sincerely wrong while thinking they are sincerely right.

History has shown that the reality of the Holy Spirit has been easily overlooked for centuries. This is true even among astute Bible Scholars. And then, when the truth regarding the indwelling and manifestations of the Spirit is brought to light, the carnal mind tends to reject it. Satan fights this truth vehemently because he knows how expedient and necessary it is to Christ.

Had Dad only known it, the Holy Spirit had taken up residence within him at the time of his conversion. Although the Holy Spirit is given to everyone who believes, the Spirit is immediately quenched in many cases because of ignorance, peer pressure, and even unbelief. Sound teaching is needed almost everywhere.

Rejection of the truth can become one's downfall, in which case, the light in them becomes darkness. They may have been born into this darkness, or have been led into it by others. They may be confronted with opportunities to come out of it, but others will not come out with them, therefore they remain in darkness.

- *LUK 11:35 Take heed therefore that the light which is in thee be not darkness.*

36 If thy whole body therefore be full of light, having no part dark, the whole shall be full of light, as when the bright shining of a candle doth give thee light.

The truth became light in my dad, but it became darkness in the hired hand because he opposed it. The light of truth which we have can become darkness if we take a position opposing that truth. Many people have done this concerning the Holy Ghost and the manifestation of his gifts. This is a terrible tragedy.

- *MAT 6:23 ... If therefore the light that is in thee be darkness, how great is that darkness!*

It is with great concern that I approach the subject of this book, hoping I will not appear to think I am more spiritual than someone who has not experienced some gift of the Spirit. I merely want to encourage them to go on to the fullness, and not stop short of tasting all of God's goodness and blessings.

- *EPH 3:16 That he would grant you, according to the riches of his glory, to be strengthened with might by his Spirit in the inner man ...*
  19 ... And to know the love of Christ, which passeth knowledge, that ye might be filled with all the fulness of God.

I have a natural tendency to want to share with others anything good that I discover. I am always encouraging my wife to taste something that seems delicious to me, and I believe will taste good to her ... if she will try it. When she shares the pleasure with me, it is a great experience to feel I have introduced her to something that adds a little larger dimension to our mutual experience and knowledge. In return, she enjoys the same excitement about sharing with me her blessings and discoveries.

On the other hand, if I offer her something she is already convinced she does not like, or she just does not like the looks of it, her reaction can be completely different. If I continue to urge her to try something new that she is rejecting from prior experience, or sheer visual dislike, it must be done with caution, lest my persistence become irritating.

When I am successful in getting her to go ahead and try anyway, and with eyebrow-raising surprise she registers her approval, I am pleasantly thankful for her being able to override her rejection, and dare to try, even against her will, something that I knew was good, and would be good to her.

I believe there is something wonderful to be shared about the Holy Spirit and speaking in other tongues as the Spirit gives the utterance. There is no pride involved on my part, no ego, no pushiness, and no utter motive, nothing to gain on my part except the joy of sharing.

Turned off

It cannot be denied that some Pentecostals have come across as pushy and egotistical. If anyone reading has ever thought that those who are excited about the baptism in the Holy Ghost feel they are better, or more spiritual, please do not hold that against them. I am sure there are some who feel that way, or at least have given that impression. But, I truly believe, that from my experience with many thousands, almost none truly feel better, or more superior, and they have no intention of giving that impression. Their zeal may have exceeded their wisdom and knowledge.

It is obvious that some feel a compelling responsibility to get out the good news about the fullness of the Spirit. They are so thrilled with their own personal experience, and are so totally convinced concerning its importance to all believers, that they are often received as strong-willed, overbearing, or riding a hobbyhorse.

On the other hand, people have been accused of being pushy and egotistical, when they honestly have not been so. Those who think they are being pushed can be extremely defensive about their religious beliefs. Protectiveness and self-preservation takes over at the mention of anything new, different, or already rejected. Communication is usually broken before any complete or coherent idea can be explained. The result is that the whole story is never allowed to be given, and the whole truth is never heard.

Rudeness, silence, deaf ears, impatience, or being ignored often prevent the truth from being shared. One can also prevent the truth from entering their mind and heart by continually debating and arguing every point that is mentioned. Many walk in darkness because they cannot put themselves into a listening mode.

It is tragic for a new convert to be given the Holy Spirit when they are born again, and yet, through ignorance, or prejudice, fail to understand the fullness of the Spirit, and even argue against it, right while they are quenching the Spirit within them. This is the case with many Christians in the world today. They are living beneath their privileges. In such cases, they are not enjoying all the benefits provided by Christ and given to the New Testament church.

One is not being better-than-thou for speaking out on these issues, any more than the preacher in the pulpit, when he speaks out against shortcomings, and challenges the congregation to go deeper with God.

One must avoid taking a noncommittal position concerning the gifts of the Spirit by saying, "if God wants me to have it he will give it to me." This would be no different than saying, "if God wants me to be saved, he will save me." If one accepts being born again, as a believer, they must accept that God has given them the gift of the Holy Ghost. They must desire spiritual gifts, and believe that God will manifest the gift of tongues to them as a sign. As they read their Bibles they must search for anything that is missing or dormant in their spiritual experience, and ask God for them. Paul said *"desire spiritual gifts"* (1CO 14:1).

Hearing Jesus

It is of utmost importance when we read the Bible that we hear everything which Jesus said, and that we believe it, and obey. Great blessings are promised to those who will hear, believe, and obey.

- *ACT 5:32 And we are his witnesses of these things; and so is also the Holy Ghost, whom God hath given to them that obey him.*

Those who hear Jesus and refuse to believe and obey suffer great consequences of divine judgment and punishment. One must remember they are reading the Bible, which is the word of God, and when Jesus speaks he is speaking the word of God. The benefit of hearing Jesus and receiving that which he says is "**life everlasting**."

- *JOH 12:49 For I have not spoken of myself; but the Father which sent me, he gave me a commandment, what I should say, and what I should speak.*
  50 And I know that his commandment is life everlasting: whatsoever I speak therefore, even as the Father said unto me, so I speak.

Just before the above verses Jesus said the following:

- *JOH 12:47 And if any man hear my words, and believe not, I judge him not: for I came not to judge the world, but to save the world.*

48 He that rejecteth me, and receiveth not my words, hath one that judgeth him: the word that I have spoken, the same shall judge him in the last day.

In the context of this book you are reading, it is seriously consequential that one hear Jesus clearly when he speaks. A terrible default occurs when one hears, but they fail to actually hear … or they misunderstand.

- *MAT 13:13 Therefore speak I to them in parables: because they seeing see not; and hearing they hear not, neither do they understand.*
  14 And in them is fulfilled the prophecy of Esaias, which saith, By hearing ye shall hear, and shall not understand; and seeing ye shall see, and shall not perceive:
  15 For this people's heart is waxed gross, and their ears are dull of hearing, and their eyes they have closed; lest at any time they should see with their eyes and hear with their ears, and should understand with their heart, and should be converted, and I should heal them.

In regards to the Holy Spirit, it is important to hear <u>and understand</u> everything which Jesus said.

When Jesus and some of his disciples were on the mount of transfiguration, God spoke from a cloud:

- *MAT 17:5 While he yet spake, behold, a bright cloud overshadowed them: and behold a voice out of the cloud, which said, This is my beloved Son, in whom I am well pleased; **<u>hear ye him</u>**.*
  6 And when the disciples heard it, they fell on their face, and were sore afraid.

We should experience the same awesome fear concerning hearing Jesus when he speaks … fear lest we should fail to hear and understand. Jesus said much concerning the Holy Ghost, which is disregarded by many, or discarded, disbelieved, ignored, rejected or misunderstood.

Jesus said the following:

- *MAR 4:9 And he said unto them, He that hath ears to hear, let him hear.*
- *JOH 14:23 Jesus answered and said unto him, If a man love me, he will keep my words: and my Father will love him, and we will come unto him, and make our abode with him.*

The following are some extremely important words which were spoken by Jesus regarding the Holy Ghost.

- *JOH 14:26 But the Comforter, which is the Holy Ghost, whom the Father will send in my name, he shall teach you all things, and bring all things to your remembrance, whatsoever I have said unto you.*
  27 Peace I leave with you, my peace I give unto you: not as the world giveth, give I unto you. Let not your heart be troubled, neither let it be afraid.
- *JOH 16:13 Howbeit when he, the Spirit of truth, is come, he will guide you into all truth: for he shall not speak of himself; but whatsoever he shall hear, that shall he speak: and he will shew you things to come.*
  14 He shall glorify me: for he shall receive of mine, and shall shew it unto you.
  15 All things that the Father hath are mine: therefore said I, that he shall take of mine, and shall shew it unto you.

- *MAR 16:17 And these signs shall follow them that believe; In my name shall they cast out devils; they shall speak with new tongues;*

The Apostle Paul wrote to the Corinthian Church concerning speaking in other tongues:

- *1CO 14:20 Brethren, be not children in understanding: howbeit in malice be ye children, but in understanding be men.*
  21 In the law it is written, With men of other tongues and other lips will I speak unto this people; and yet for all that will they not hear me, saith the Lord.
  22 Wherefore tongues are for a sign, not to them that Believe, but to them that believe not: but prophesying serveth not for them that believe not, but for them which believe.

Speaking in other tongues (foreign languages) was a convincing miracle on the day of Pentecost. It was so convincing that over three thousand souls were converted to faith in Jesus because foreigners from fifteen different countries heard their own native language being supernaturally spoken by ordinary Jews.

Keep reading this book "ABOUT THE HOLY SPIRIT," because you will read about incidents where this has occurred in recent times.

The pure and simple truth is that Jesus believed in the Holy Ghost dwelling in the body-temple of his Christian followers. One must be extremely ready to hear and believe the words of Jesus … who believed in the Holy Ghost, and believed in speaking with tongues by the utterance of the Holy Ghost.

Laying on of hands

The Apostle Paul exercised a strong influence on a young man named Timothy. It is evident that Timothy received the baptism in the Holy Ghost when Paul, in company with some other ministers (*the presbytery*) laid hands on him, which gives evidenced in scripture as one of the ways God gives the gift of the Holy Ghost.

- *ACT 8:14 Now when the apostles which were at Jerusalem heard that Samaria had received the word of God, they sent unto them Peter and John:*
  15 Who, when they were come down, prayed for them, that they might receive the Holy Ghost:
  16 (For as yet he was fallen upon none of them: only they were baptized in the name of the Lord Jesus.)
  17 <u>Then laid they their hands on them, and they received the Holy Ghost.</u>

The <u>GIFT</u> of the Holy Spirit

In the New Testament the Holy Spirit is called a "<u>**Gift**</u> from God."

- *ACT 2:38 Then Peter said unto them, Repent, and be baptized every one of you in the name of Jesus Christ for the remission of sins, and ye shall receive the **gift** of the Holy Ghost.*

When Peter preached at the home of Cornelius, and while he was preaching, the Holy Ghost fell on all who were in the room. The Holy Ghost is called a "gift."

- *ACT 10:45 And they of the circumcision which believed were astonished, as many as came with Peter, because that on the Gentiles also was poured out the **gift** of the Holy Ghost.*
46 For they heard them speak with tongues, and magnify God.

Two Letters which Paul wrote to Timothy are recorded as Books in the New Testament. In both letters Paul advised Timothy to give special attention to the **gift**, which was the Holy Spirit which he had received.

Paul told Timothy to *"Neglect not the **gift**,"* and *"stir up the **gift**."*

The First Letter

- *1TI 4:13 Till I come, give attendance to reading, to exhortation, to doctrine.*
*14 Neglect not the **gift** that is in thee, which was given thee by prophecy, with the laying on of the hands of the presbytery.*
15 Meditate upon these things; give thyself wholly to them; that thy profiting may appear to all.
16 Take heed unto thyself, and unto the doctrine; continue in them: for in doing this thou shalt both save thyself, and them that hear thee.

The Second Letter

- *2TI 1:6 Wherefore I put thee in remembrance that thou stir up the **gift** of God, which is in thee by the putting on of my hands.*
7 For God hath not given us the spirit of fear; but of power, and of love, and of a sound mind.

By receiving the **gift** of the Holy Ghost Timothy had been given the Spirit *"of power, and of love, and of a sound mind."*

The **gifts** (plural) of the Holy Spirit are given to every person as a means to bless others with a spiritual ministry, through an ability that only God can give.

- *1PE 4:10 As every man hath received the **gift**, even so minister the same one to another, as good stewards of the manifold grace of God.*
  11 If any man speak, let him speak as the oracles of God; if any man minister, let him do it as of the ability which God giveth: that God in all things may be glorified through Jesus Christ, to whom be praise and dominion for ever and ever. Amen.

When someone gives a gift, it is appropriate to thank the giver warmly, and to express appreciation for their thoughtfulness. When God himself is the giver of the **gift**, how much more are expressions of thanksgiving appropriate and proper. The magnificence of the **gift** of the Holy Ghost should be appreciated above all other gifts, even if the gifts be diamonds or elaborate Jewels of gold and silver.

Those who know the truth, based on the word of God, will be able to estimate the value of the Holy Spirit, and will not hide him away behind a closed door. The Holy Spirit will be revealed through a continuance of worship, and his beauty extolled through praise and magnification. The Holy Spirit is the greatest, most adorable, most magnanimous **gift** known to man, and to God.

The first thing Jesus did after he returned to heaven, and sat down by his Father in his throne, was to send the **gift** of the Holy Ghost back to dwell in the bodies of all his disciples on the earth.

- *EPH 4:7 But unto every one of us is given grace according to the measure of the gift of Christ.*

*8 Wherefore he saith, When he ascended up on high, he led captivity captive, **and gave gifts unto men**.*

The Holy Spirit is a gift from God above," who made up his mind …"out of his own will," to give the gift of the Holy Spirit to his children …"as a kind of firstfruits," because of his Fatherly love.

- *JAM 1:16 Do not err, my beloved brethren.*
  17 Every good gift and <u>every perfect gift is from above</u>, and cometh down from the Father of lights, with whom is no variableness, neither shadow of turning.
  *18 **Of his own will** begat he us with the word of truth, that we should be <u>a kind of firstfruits</u> of his creatures.*

Remember, the gifts of the Spirit are exactly what they are called – "GIFTS." And they are from the Heavenly Father through his Son, Jesus Christ, himself. They are marvelous and to be desired. Paul said, *"desire spiritual gifts (1 CO 14:1)."*

There is never anything wrong with asking God for something that may not be present, or manifest in one's life, even though it is a free gift. I would say to anyone, if you have not received the manifestation of a gift that has been promised to you, ask for it … boldly. Go to the throne of grace and find out why you do not have it, and get it by faith. Ask others to pray with you … *"earnestly contend for the faith once delivered to the saints"* (JUD 1:3) … *"resist the devil"* (JAM 4:7), who does not want you to enjoy the gifts and blessings of God.

Jesus foretold about speaking in tongues

The last words which Jesus spoke before he ascended back to heaven had to do with the supernatural gifts of the spirit that would be manifested through his disciples as they continued to minister in his name. This is important because they are the parting words of Jesus. In my Bible the following verses are printed in red, meaning they are the exact words of Jesus, and stand out on the page:

- *MAR 16:17 And these signs shall follow them that believe; In my name shall they cast out devils;* **<u>they shall speak with new tongues</u>***;*
  18 They shall take up serpents; and if they drink any deadly thing, it shall not hurt them; they shall lay hands on the sick, and they shall recover.

For **"*they shall speak with new tongues*"** to be among the final parting words of Jesus means it was significantly important to him. The next verses continue as follows:

- *19 So then after the Lord had spoken unto them, he was received up into heaven, and sat on the right hand of God.*
  20 And they went forth, and preached everywhere, the Lord working with them, and <u>confirming the word with signs following</u>.

Although it was not a complete list of spiritual gifts In verse 17 and 18, Jesus listed some of the supernatural things that would occur as confirmation of the word of the Lord which they would be preaching.

Chapters fourteen through seventeen of the Gospel of John give detailed information and instructions concerning the Holy Ghost. These were also last minute instructions and teachings directly from Christ and must be accepted word-for-word. The thing that matters most is not what *we* believe about the Holy Ghost and speaking in other tongues, but what *Jesus* believes. **Jesus**

believes in speaking with other tongues (foreign languages) as the Holy Spirit gives the utterance.

Speaking in other tongues simply means, "speaking in other languages," or a language "other" than the language of the speaker. Most commonly used is the phrase, *"speaking with tongues,"* appearing eight times. The words *"other tongues"* is used twice. It is understood that the speaker is making verbal utterances in a language which is completely unknown to the speaker, and is usually unknown to the audience. The exception is that on the day of Pentecost devout Jews were present from fifteen different nations who heard the Galilean disciples speaking in the native languages of the foreigners who understood what they were speaking. They knew these simple Galileans could not naturally speak in the language of this diverse assemblage of foreign Jews who were amazed.

- *ACT 2:7 And they were all amazed and marvelled, saying one to another, Behold, are not all these which speak Galilaeans?*
  8 And how hear we every man in our own tongue, wherein we were born?
  9 Parthians, and Medes, and Elamites, and the dwellers in Mesopotamia, and in Judaea, and Cappadocia, in Pontus, and Asia,
  10 Phrygia, and Pamphylia, in Egypt, and in the parts of Libya about Cyrene, and strangers of Rome, Jews and proselytes,
  11 Cretes and Arabians, **we do hear them speak in our tongues the wonderful works of God.**

Speaking with tongues is a miracle

Paul made it clear that when one speaks with tongues valid languages are being spoken. Paul used the word *"voices,"* and said they all were significant, or had a meaning somewhere in the world.

> *1CO 14:10 There are, it may be, so many kinds of voices in the world, and none of them is without signification.*
> *11 Therefore if I know not the meaning of the voice, I shall be unto him that speaketh a barbarian, and he that speaketh shall be a barbarian unto me.*

It is important to realize that when one speaks with tongues by the utterance of the Holy Ghost it is a miracle because a literal human language is being spoken which could be understood somewhere in the world.

It is of equal importance to know that one cannot speak in tongues except through utterance given by the Holy Ghost. It is not necessary to help, prime, or assist the Holy Ghost, for he is well able to give utterance without fleshly aid.

Speaking in tongues at will

The idea of "speaking in tongues at will" has practically become a doctrine with some, and has been a source of confusion. It must be clearly understood that speaking in tongues is truly supernatural, and is not done under the control of the mind or will of the person doing the speaking. They are speaking as they are given utterance by the Holy Ghost. To deviate from this rule opens the door to carnality and fleshly manipulation of what is supposed to be a totally spiritual manifestation. Anyone who is practicing this or teaching it should stop immediately, and search the word of God.

This belief has been based on an incomplete statement taken

from a very important verse. I once heard a minister encouraging people to speak in tongues at will. He coached them into going into some form of non-intelligible gibberish, actually just jabbering on their own. He kept repeating the phrase, "<u>they</u> spake with other tongues," emphasizing, "<u>they</u> spake ... <u>they</u> spake." His audience did not know he was misquoting the passage. Not one time did the minister quote the complete verse for had he done so, it would have contradicted what he was saying. Furthermore, the text does not say "they spake." Read it for yourself to see who was the source of the speaking:

- *ACT 2:4 And they were all filled with the Holy Ghost, and began to speak with other tongues, as the Spirit gave them utterance.*

It does not say, they spoke, but it says *"they were filled ... and began to speak **as the Spirit gave them utterance**."* When Jesus told his disciples that supernatural signs would follow, or accompany believers, he listed speaking with new tongues along with some other amazing supernatural gifts. Not one of these supernatural manifestations of the Spirit can be manipulated or controlled by the human mind, and this includes speaking with new tongues.

The people on the day of Pentecost were not speaking from the source of their own mind, but were speaking from a supernatural source of utterance. All who were speaking in other tongues were Galileans (Jews who lived in Galilee). These Galileans knew only their native language and yet a phenomenal miracle was occurring. There was no manipulation of the manifestation because it was a total surprise to all of them. The one receiving the Holy Ghost did not have the slightest notion, or preconceived idea that this phenomenon would occur. This supernatural sign was strictly from God, and not from their minds. The foreigners who were present in Jerusalem knew these simple people would not be able to do this, except by a miracle.

Every effort has been made to reduce what happened on the day of Pentecost to nothing more than what these simple Galileans could do in the natural. I heard another person misquoting the Bible and he honestly was not aware of it.

He kept quoting these words, "they spake in their own tongue wherein they were born." He was so positive the Bible said this, it was impossible to convince him, even by showing, that the Bible did not say such. He finally settled on Acts 2:6 as his proof that the Gentiles were speaking in their own language. This verse is as follows:

- *ACT 2:6 Now when this was noised abroad, the multitude came together, and were confounded, because that every man heard them speak in his own language.*

It was contended that "his" referred to the one doing the speaking. Of course it was the multitude which heard their own language. Common sense shows there would be nothing so exciting about a Galilean speaking in his own language, that great crowds would come together to hear him? There were Galileans all over town speaking in the language of the Galileans and it brought no crowds together.

But when a man from Cappadocia, or Asia, or Mesopotamia, in passing by, happened to hear someone speaking his language, it certainly caught his attention -- to hear his own language being spoken in Jerusalem by a Galilean who was a non-scholar.

One can be sure that he would turn aside to find what was going on. The first startling thing was to hear the Galilean glorifying and praising Jesus Christ as the only begotten of the Father, crucified, risen, ascended, and now at the right hand of the Father as head of his kingdom.

After fifty days of almost total silence from the followers of Jesus, Most all religious Jews were certain that this "Jesus business" had been silenced forever. But now, these simple Galileans are speaking of him, and to him, powerfully, and of all things, in the languages of the foreigners?

One can imagine how this amazed the foreign Jew, half-believing ... half-disbelieving ... as he rushed out to tell others what he had just witnessed. It did not take long, in those days of news by word-of-mouth for a massive crowd to gather. These religious Jews crowded around because they knew they were hearing and witnessing a miracle, so much that from that crowd three thousand became believer in Christ, and were baptized in the Holy Ghost ... which was the baptism Jesus said was coming, and it did come on the day of Pentecost. Jesus had said in verse 5, *"but ye shall be baptized with the Holy Ghost not many days hence."*

- *ACT 2:41 Then they that gladly received his word were baptized: and the same day there were added unto them about three thousand souls.*

"Baptized" could not possibly be a reference to water baptism, because the emphasis of that day was on the "Baptism in the Holy Ghost."

When these foreign Jews from fifteen different countries heard Galileans speaking in their native foreign language by the utterance of the Holy Ghost, this was convincing evidence that a miracle was occurring, and they believed in Jesus, and were also convinced concerning the reality of the Holy Ghost.

- *ACT 2:7 And they were all amazed and marvelled, saying one to another, Behold, are not all these which speak Galilaeans? 8 And how hear we every man in our own tongue, wherein we were born?*

Verse eight settles the matter. Make no mistake, speaking in other languages by the utterance of the Holy Ghost is a miracle, and this truth must be upheld if the integrity of speaking in tongues is to remain intact.

Today, some who suppress the idea of speaking in other tongues suggest that after the Holy Ghost fell on the one hundred and twenty believers, they went out into the streets and began to witness to these religious Jewish men who were in Jerusalem to celebrate the feast of Pentecost.

There is no indication that the disciples went out into the street at all. They did not go to the multitudes, the multitudes came to them. They certainly were not witnessing in the common sense of the term. Most assuredly, they were witnessing to the greatness of God and magnifying Christ, but they were doing it in languages other than their own. They had no idea what they were saying, because it was not in their own language.

- *1CO 14:14 For if I pray in an unknown tongue, my spirit prayeth, but my understanding is unfruitful.*

Paul clearly taught that when one is speaking or praying in other tongues by the utterance of the Holy Ghost, it is the Holy Spirit praying through their submitted human spirit ... during which their understanding is unfruitful. It is not them speaking, but the Holy Ghost. This fact has already been established from the scripture:

- *ACT 2:4 And they were all filled with the Holy Ghost, and begin to speak with other tongues, <u>as the Spirit gave them utterance</u>.*

"AS THE SPIRIT GAVE THEM UTTERANCE" should be kept as a cardinal watchword, and speaking in tongues should never be reduced to something that can be done by the will, or discretion of a person.

The Comforter

The giving of the Holy Ghost has important significance to God the Father, and to Jesus, his Son, or else it would not have happened. The Holy Ghost was sent to the church ten days after Christ ascended back to the Father.

Jesus had told his disciples he was not going to leave them alone after his departure, but would comfort their loneliness by requesting the Father to send the Holy Ghost to dwell within them. The comfort of having the physical presence of Christ would be replaced by the indwelling presence of the Holy Ghost as their comforter. Those who have received him to this extent of personal reality testify to the comforting presence of the Holy Ghost.

- *JOH 14:16 And I will pray the Father, and he shall give you another **Comforter**, <u>that he may abide with you for ever</u>;*
- *JOH 16:7 Nevertheless I tell you the truth; It is expedient for you that I go away: for if I go not away, the **Comforter** will not come unto you; but if I depart, I will send him unto you.*

Jesus told his disciples that the Holy Ghost would not depart, or go back to the Father, but would remain with them until the end of the world. This gives clear indication that the Holy Ghost was not given only to the early disciples, because they certainly would not live until the end of the world. Peter quoted that the Holy Ghost was given to *"them who are afar off, even as many as the Lord our God shall call."* We today are included -- we are afar off from them -- and are called by the Lord unto salvation.

People who truly understand the importance of the indwelling of the Holy Spirit openly welcome him into their hearts and lives. They are extremely appreciative of his comfort in times of need and are grateful for his intercession before God on their behalf. They relish those times when the Spirit assists them in praise and worship before God and his Christ. They soon became aware of those situations when he gives them wisdom and knowledge in dealing with their daily problems of life when the right decision is critical. The Holy Spirit becomes to them exactly what Jesus said he would be ... a Comforter and Guide. And, of great importance is how he reveals truth from the word of God.

- *JOH 14:26 But the Comforter, which is the Holy Ghost, whom the Father will send in my name, he shall teach you all things, and bring all things to your remembrance, whatsoever I have said unto you.*
- *JOH 16:13 Howbeit when he, the Spirit of truth, is come, he will guide you into all truth: for he shall not speak of himself; but whatsoever he shall hear, that shall he speak: and he will shew you things to come.*
  14 He shall glorify me: for he shall receive of mine, and shall shew it unto you.
  15 All things that the Father hath are mine: therefore said I, that he shall take of mine, and shall shew it unto you.

9

Prophesy About Speaking in Other Tongues

The earliest mention of speaking in other tongues is found in a prophesy by Isaiah.

- *ISA 28:9 Whom shall he teach knowledge? and whom shall he make to understand doctrine? Them that are weaned from the milk, and drawn from the breasts.*
  10 For precept must be upon precept, precept upon precept; line upon line, line upon line; here a little, and there a little:
  *11 **For with stammering lips and another tongue will he speak to this people**.*
  12 To whom he said, This is the rest wherewith ye may cause the weary to rest; and this is the refreshing: yet they would not hear.

This is an amazing prophesy. It is clearly the responsibility of the Holy Ghost to teach knowledge and to give the understanding of doctrine (v. 9). Those who do not want to leave the milk of the word have a hard time dealing with the doctrines concerning the Holy Ghost, and like an infant, they want to stay with the breast. The *"strong meat"* of the word is more than they can digest (HEB 5:14).

The Holy Spirit is the Teacher

Isaiah asks *"whom shall he teach knowledge? and to whom shall he make to understand doctrine?"* The Biblical answer is "only those who are in a correct spiritual relationship with Christ can be taught by the Holy Spirit." No other teacher is qualified to place *"precept upon precept"* and *"line upon line"* ... to take a truth from the word of God in one place *("here a little")*, and then from another place *("there a little")*, and *"rightly divide"* the word of God to reveal the truth of the Bible.

- *2TI 2:15 Study to shew thyself approved unto God, a workman that needeth not to be ashamed, <u>rightly dividing</u> the word of truth.*

Isaiah was given a prophetic view of New Testament believers, those *"to whom he would teach knowledge ... and make to understand doctrine."* He identified them as those who speak *"with stammering lips and another tongue."* It is evident Isaiah prophetically saw New Testament Christians who were baptized in the Holy Spirit and who spoke in other tongues. This is clearly the way he identified them as the one to whom God would teach knowledge and make to understand doctrine. This does not exclude any believer, because all who are born again have received the Holy Ghost. If they have not spoken in tongues, that is not the fault of God, or of Jesus, or of the Holy Ghost. And, it may not be their fault alone. Many Christians are functioning in environments that hide those truths from them. Therefore, ignorance of the truth concerning this matter can be the problem. Of course there are those who have outright rejected this truth and have willfully chosen to refuse the knowledge or the experience.

The Holy Spirit Teaches <u>All Truth</u>

- *JOH 16:13 Howbeit when he, the Spirit of truth, is come, <u>he will guide you into **all truth**</u>: for he shall not speak of himself; but whatsoever he shall hear, that shall he speak: and he will shew you things to come.*
  14 He shall glorify me: for he shall receive of mine, and shall shew it unto you.
  15 <u>All things</u> that the Father hath are mine: therefore said I, that he shall take of mine, and shall shew it unto you.

The Holy Ghost has full access to *"all"* the knowledge of Christ who has access to the full knowledge of his heavenly Father. Jesus explained, in the above statement, the limitless knowledge of truth to which we have access through the Holy Ghost ... *"all truth."*

Therefore, The Holy Ghost, as the designated divine teacher of the word of God -- since he wrote the book -- is qualified to put it *"precept upon precept, line upon line,"* and to rightly divide it *"here a little and there a little."* A key passage is as follows:

- *2PE 1:21 For the prophecy came not in old time by the will of man: but holy men of God spake as <u>they were moved by the Holy Ghost</u>.*

Paul placed much emphasis on the direct inspiration of the word of God.

- *2TI 3:16 All scripture is given by inspiration of God, and is profitable for doctrine, for reproof, for correction, for instruction in righteousness:*
  17 That the man of God may be perfect, throughly furnished unto all good works.

Any knowledge about Christ, truth, or the gifts of the spirit comes only through the Holy Ghost. Whatever one learns should be cherished and carefully guarded. It must first be gained, and then kept.

- *2TI 1:14 That good thing which was committed unto thee <u>keep</u> by the Holy Ghost which dwelleth in us.*

Surely Paul had this in mind when he told Timothy to *"study to show thyself approved unto God, a workman that needeth not to be ashamed, rightly dividing the word of truth"* (2 TIM 2:15).

When the truth is spoken, then that truth must be revealed by the Holy Spirit before the hearers can receive it into their heart. Truth is first received into the mind, and there it is considered, then accepted or rejected. When a person does not allow the Holy Spirit to control or teach, truth can be rejected by the carnal, fleshly, logical, reasoning mind.

Some will not believe

God gave the Old Testament prophet, Isaiah, a truly supernatural revelation of how things would be in the church age. God chose to show him a glimpse of speaking in other tongues, and that it would be a spiritually restful and refreshing experience for believers to possess the Holy Ghost as an indwelling Spirit. God also showed him that even after giving all this, yet some would not hear.

- *ISA 28:11 For with stammering lips and another tongue will he speak to this people.*

> *12 To whom he said, This is the rest wherewith ye may cause
> the weary to rest; and this is the refreshing: <u>yet they would
> not hear</u>.*

Many people become uneasy at the mention of the Holy
Ghost, and have difficulty accepting speaking in other tongues.
Some cannot deny the Biblical authenticity of the Holy Ghost
and the accompanying gifts, but they place the demonstration
and operation of spiritual gifts under such stringent regulations
that the chance of the manifestation of tongues or any other gift
ever happening in their life is practically nil ... and they strongly
influence others around them to also suppress the Holy Spirit.

God had spoken through the Prophet Isaiah, *"with another
tongue will I speak unto this people."* He then said, *"and this is the
refreshing wherewith I will cause the weary to be refreshed."*

What better confirmation could there be than to quote God
himself? What more could we ask today as scriptural proof for
believing in the miracle of speaking in other tongues as the Spirit
gives the utterance? How could anyone reject such a thrilling
experience?

If God called it a *"refreshing,"* it certainly merits special
attention. Yet, God sadly injected, *"in spite of this, some will not
believe."*

Early and latter rain

Joel prophesied concerning the outpouring of the Holy Spirit
and compared it to the early and latter rain. He was referring to
spring rain that comes during the time of planting that is necessary
for germination of seed (early rain), and then to the summer rain
(latter rain) that is needed to cause development of plants and the
production of fruit and seed in the pod, making ready for harvest.

- *JOE 2:23 Be glad then, ye children of Zion, and rejoice in the LORD your God: for he hath given you the former rain moderately, and he will cause to come down for you the rain, the former rain, and the latter rain ....*
  24 And the floors shall be full of wheat, and the fats shall overflow with wine and oil ...
  26 And ye shall eat in plenty, and be satisfied, and praise the name of the LORD your God, that hath dealt wondrously with you: and my people shall never be ashamed.

The "former rain moderately" found its significance on the day of Pentecost. The main thrust of Joel's prophesy had to do with the latter rain, the big rain which finishes off the crop. Joel's prophesy indicated that the first rain was a moderate rain in comparison to the latter rain ... an abundant outpouring of the Holy Spirit which would occur in the last days just prior to the second coming of Christ.

This amazing latter rain occurs as the response to the great tribulation which Satan serves against Christians as his last shot against Christ through the Antichrist. The greatest Christian revival occurs in opposition to the Devil and the Antichrist, and Jesus shortens the days of the the great tribulation by ending it with his second coming and the first resurrection of all sainted dead.

Pentecost not the last day outpouring

On the day of Pentecost, Peter did not say that which was occurring right then was the fulfillment of the prophesy of Joel, but he said, *"this is that which was spoken by the prophet Joel."* Then Peter quotes about the great outpouring which would occur in the last days.

Correlating this with other scriptures concerning the end time establishes that there shall be a definite *"last days"* just prior to the second coming of Christ that shall be characterized by a mighty outpouring of the Holy Ghost. God has plans for a huge harvest in the end time and the outpouring of the Holy Ghost plays a big part in it. The Holy Ghost was poured out on the day of Pentecost, but that was not the last days outpouring. That was *"the former rain moderately"* (JOE 2:25).

Before the great and notable day

This outpouring will, without doubt, occur *"before the great and notable day of the Lord come."* Now here is the point: Joel prophesied -- over eight hundred years before Christ -- concerning a great outpouring of the Holy Spirit that would come from God in the last days. An initial outpouring was given to the church on the day of Pentecost, with the explanation, *"this is that"* (the same experience of being filled with the Holy Spirit) which will be poured out during the last days.

Upon all flesh

The **last days** outpouring shall be of such proportions that it is said, *"I will pour out my Spirit upon **all flesh**."* This gives reason to pay special attention to the matter of being filled with the Holy Spirit.

It is *"sound doctrine"* to state that, since the day of Pentecost, every one who repents and is placed into Christ *(baptized into Christ)* receives the outpouring of the Holy Spirit and should walk in the fullness of the experience.

- *ACT 2:38 Then Peter said unto them, Repent, and be baptized every one of you in the name of Jesus Christ for the remission of sins, <u>and ye shall receive the gift of the Holy Ghost.</u>*
  39 For the promise is unto you, and to your children, and to all that are afar off, even as many as the Lord our God shall call.

One should not allow their natural inhibitions to prevent the supernatural manifestations from freely occurring. Jesus said the Holy Ghost would abide with his followers *"for ever."*

- *JOH 14:16 And I will pray the Father, and he shall give you another Comforter, <u>that he may abide with you for ever;</u>*
  17 Even the Spirit of truth; whom the world cannot receive, because it seeth him not, neither knoweth him: but ye know him; for he dwelleth with you, and shall be in you.

No Christian is exempt from this indwelling of the Holy Spirit, because He is given to every person who is born again.

When one buys an automobile they can pick the equipment they want -- air conditioner, electric door locks, power antenna, power windows, etc. The Holy Ghost is not an embellishment like fancy hubcaps ... *"take it or leave it."* The infilling of the Holy Ghost is not optional equipment. He comes with the package just like a steering wheel comes with an automobile, and is just as necessary.

Today, if you get Jesus, you get the Holy Ghost which he said he would send from the Father immediately upon arriving back into heaven.

- *JOH 16:7 Nevertheless I tell you the truth; It is expedient for you that I go away: for if I go not away, the Comforter will not come unto you; but if I depart, I will send him unto you.*

The following verse should establish forever that the Holy Ghost is given to <u>everyone</u> who calls upon Christ in obedience.

- *ACT 5:32 And we are his witnesses of these things; and so is also the Holy Ghost, whom God hath given to them that obey him.*

The Turn of the Twentieth Century

Historically, truth regarding the baptism with the Holy Spirit was smothered and lost by the church as grievous wolves entered the flock, beginning with the end of the first century. This was predicted by the apostle Paul.

- *ACT 20:29 For I know this, that after my departing shall grievous wolves enter in among you, not sparing the flock.*
30 Also of your own selves shall men arise, speaking perverse things, to draw away disciples after them.
31 Therefore watch, and remember, that by the space of three years I ceased not to warn every one night and day with tears.

The resultant decline of truth in the church brought on by these wolves led to the loss of most cardinal truths. Justification by faith totally disappeared from the scene as these false teachers replaced grace with their pagan works. The eventual takeover of the church by Constantine in the fourth century led to various religious teachers throughout the centuries who are falsely revered by many as renowned scholars. Opponents of speaking in tongues point out that these historical scholars never mentioned the baptism in the Holy Spirit in a Pentecostal sense. To these opponents this is positive proof that tongues ceased from the church soon after the original apostles died off.

The fact is, through these mistakenly revered Fathers almost all truth was lost as the church faded into dismal darkness for centuries. This caused the entire world to sink into the dark ages which is a historical fact.

When Martin Luther rediscovered the truth regarding justification by faith as opposed to the Catholic works for righteousness, such as penance that had been imposed on Christian religion, did the light of truth begin to shine again.

Added to this was the revelation given to John Wesley that God expects followers of Christ to live in holiness and sanctification as an inseparable result of the new birth. And then more emergence of truth occurred when the light of the baptism with the Holy Spirit began to shine again, along with understanding concerning the fruit of the Spirit and the reality of the gifts of the Spirit, including speaking with other tongues as the Spirit gives utterance.

Resistance to Speaking in Tongues

Why is speaking in tongues not allowed today by many denominations, ministers, and leaders who claim to have been baptized in the Spirit? The answer is basically a historical one. Just prior to the turn of the twentieth century a sovereign work of God occurred wherein the manifestation of the gift of tongues was poured out on churches and groups of believers within a short period of time at different points around the world.

By this time the church had evolved into many divergent denominational groups who legislated the boundaries of beliefs allowed for their constituents. As could be expected, these traditional religious groups began to experience spontaneous Holy Spirit fires blazing up within their ranks, and most resisted it because it did not fit into their prescribed orthodox doctrinal dogma.

This original outpouring which spread around the world seems to have started in a church on Azusa Street in Los Angeles. Visitors to the three-year long revival took the message with them to various separate locations, mostly remote and isolated from each other. The spreading fire was not the results of promotions by men because there was little or no contact or communication between the various groups which could have enabled them to coordinate the timing of this outstanding event. It was not until a considerable time later that the close proximity of timing was discovered. Each group which had experienced the outpouring, believed it to be a repeat and continuation of Pentecost. The near-simultaneous **global outpouring** gives evidence that it was a sovereign work of God.

The recipients of the outpouring searched the word of God to confirm its Biblical soundness. Much to their delight they confirmed the exact experience in the Bible and believed they had rediscovered a serious void and oversight in their contemporary theology concerning the baptism in the Holy Ghost. They concluded that the baptism in the Holy Ghost which they were presently receiving had been given to the first century Church in like manner on the day of Pentecost. There was no reason that it should not continue as a normal practice of the church until Jesus comes. There was no reason to condemn these Biblical outpourings which were occurring in their day.

This spiritual phenomenon spread like a prairie fire as many Spirit filled evangelists spanned the globe sharing the word of God regarding the rediscovery of this wonderful truth that had always been in the Bible, and especially in the New Testament revelation which introduced Christ as the Baptizer in the Holy Ghost. John the Baptist, the forerunner of Christ, introduced Jesus as the one who would baptize them with the Holy Ghost.

- *MAT 3:11 I indeed baptize you with water unto repentance: but he that cometh after me is mightier than I, whose shoes I am not worthy to bear: he shall baptize you with the Holy Ghost, and with fire:*

Jesus Said:

- *LUK 24:49 And, behold, I send the promise of my Father upon you: but tarry ye in the city of Jerusalem, until ye be endued with power from on high.*

Unpremeditated -- Unmanipulated

While the early church waited in Jerusalem for the coming of the Holy Ghost, as promised by Jesus, they did not have the slightest ideas what form this experience would take. Speaking in other tongues was a totally involuntary surprise, and there was no pre-programming on the part of Jesus. Human effort, knowledge, or ingenuity had nothing to do with the manifestation of tongues which was a sovereign operation of God confirming the arrival of the Holy Spirit who had taken up his abode within them. The outpouring at the turn of the twentieth century saw the same thing happen -- totally involuntary and unpremeditated. The flame of enthusiasm spread rapidly.

Doctrine based on human experience

Several major mistakes were made at the turn of the century when the Holy Ghost was poured out. Pentecostals based their doctrine of a second or third experience on what had happened to them rather than going strictly by the Bible. Doctrine is not established by human or personal experience, but by the word of God.

The author's walk of faith

I was raised in The Church of God, a Pentecostal denomination, with headquarters in Cleveland, Tennessee. My teen years were spent living in Cleveland. We lived about five blocks from the General Offices of the denomination. The denominational High School Academy, Junior College and Bible College were about three blocks from our home. My close friends were the children of the denominational officials.

I graduated from the Academy and completed my freshman year at the Junior College. I participated in almost every extracurricular activity offered which included singing in the Lee College Quartet, president of the college choir, president of the high school senior class, president of the Beta Club, captain of the College Freshmen volleyball team, played on the basketball and football teams, both in high school and college, and was elected to "Who's Who in American Colleges and Universities."

My mother was a college English professor, and retired after twenty seven years at Lee College. My Father graduated from the Bible College several years previously which brought us to the school originally.

Needless to say, I was born and bred Church of God and cut my teeth on Church of God benches as mom and dad were in church faithfully every time the door opened. My father was an ordained minister of the Church of God denomination.

I was deeply ingrained in all the Church of God doctrines, and especially believed, along with my peers, that one had not received the Holy Ghost until they had spoken in other tongues. Hardly a church service occurred in those days without the opportunity being given for one to testify. A testimony would frequently include the following: "I am glad I am saved, sanctified, filled with the Holy Ghost with the evidence of speaking in other tongues, and have seen the light on the great Church of God."

David and Goliath

I became the pastor of the Childress, Texas, local Church of God at age nineteen in the year of nineteen hundred and fifty three. I thought I knew our doctrines well and one of my first encounters was with the pastor of the largest church in town. I met him by chance at a local automobile repair shop. He had pastored that church for thirty years and could spot a stranger in town a mile away.

I am sure I looked like a prospective church member, and he began to make my acquaintance only to learn I was the new pastor at the little Pentecostal church. He began to subtly antagonize this new kid on the block in front of several people who knew him well. He was making sport of me when he asked, "Well son, what do you preach down there at that little church?"

My zeal knew no limits and I was ready to take him on, if that is what it took to defend our gospel which I felt was being challenged. I stated that I preached that one must be saved, sanctified, and believe in being filled with the Holy Ghost, with the initial evidence of speaking in other tongues as the Spirit gives the utterance, and then should join the Church of God.

He quizzed, "so you preach that speaking in other tongues is the 'initial evidence' of being baptized in the Holy Ghost." I proudly responded, "I sure do." He then asked, "Where is the term 'initial evidence' found in the Bible?"

I said, "I don't know the exact location, but I will find it for you and let you know." He then said, "son, don't waste your time because it is not in there." I put up a little hedging argument because he seemed so dominantly positive, but I thought, "it has to be in there because I've heard it all my life. I'll find it"!

He then said, "Preacher, I'll tell you what I will do. If you can show me where that is located in the Bible, I will come join your church and let you baptize me in water; in fact, I will stand before your congregation and eat my Bible page by page."

Of course, everyone around laughed and haw-hawed real big. I knew right then I was going to really study so I could prove what we believed. This was just my first encounter with the rude awakening that I, too, could possibly be caught up in doctrines and traditions of men simply because I was born into it.

This preacher was on a roll and the crowd increased as mechanics and office personnel began to gather around for the kill! I tried to think of some excuse to walk away but he would not let me. He kept firing loaded questions at me, with each one bringing a response of laughter from the crowd.

Each question took on a deeper tone of sarcasm as he quizzed, "what goes on down there ... do you heal the sick? What percentage gets healed? Do you pray for the sick in every service? Are there any local people that we know who have been healed? I would like to visit them and check it out. When was the last time someone got healed? Was it healings like the Bible -- blind eyes, deaf ears, crippled limbs"?

He continued, "you know, I have a responsibility as a local pastor to check these claims out, for the protection of my flock that I pastor."

My nineteen-year old head was swimming and under my breath I was praying, "God help me; get me out of here; stop this harassment! He has the advantage because he is an older man with a lot more experience ... Lord, he's probably in his sixties ... gray headed, and distinguished looking." I was not aware that ministers of his denomination are usually well-schooled in the art of debate ... having studied it in their seminaries.

But, the ordeal went on. He asked, "do you all shout and jerk and jump when the Holy Ghost comes upon you? I have heard that some jump benches and others roll all over the floor screaming and shouting to the top of their voices. They call them 'Holy Rollers.' Is that right? Doesn't it get a little scary with that invisible Ghost floating around in the church and taking hold of the people, shaking and moving them around? It seems to me it would be like a giant invisible mosquito flying around, grabbing an arm and throwing it in the air, then a leg ... jerking it into a kick. What does it feel like to have the Holy Ghost take you over"?

I knew he was exaggerating normal Pentecostal worship, and I had not experienced the excesses he described, but it would be futile to deny that such had doubtless occurred somewhere, sometime.

He then began to rail on the emotional nature of Pentecostal worship characterized by crying and laughter, worship and praising, joy and shouting. He then changed the tempo, looked me in the eye soberly like he was going to force a confession out of me, and said, "Do you shout?" Before I could answer he asked demandingly, "tell me, what makes you shout? Isn't it all just emotionalism?"

By this time I was desperately praying on the inside, "God help me! Give me something to say. I felt like I was in the lion's den. All I had done was come in this place of business to get my car worked on and had run into this.

I did not know it, but his tactic was to keep me off balance by not allowing time to answer anything before he would fire another intimidating question that was loaded to the extent that it favored his point by the way it was asked. He had the skill to answer his own questions by another rapid-fire question, or at least to make it appear there was no answer on my part. The laughter of the crowd that had become several bodies deep was roaring in my brain.

He had set me back on my heels by his first question about the *"initial evidence."* When I stepped into his trap through ignorance he had me going his way, and was successful in keeping me off balance and defensive, while he was definitely on the offense.

Answer with a question

But, when he asked the question, "what makes you shout," I felt a little surge of the Holy Ghost in my nineteen-year-old spirit. I was totally dependent upon the help of the Holy Spirit at that point, and I quickly asked, "God, what shall I say? How shall I answer"?

The Holy Ghost communicated with me, Spirit to spirit, just as real as if it had been an audible conversation, and said, "Do as Jesus did -- answer him with a question. **Ask him what makes him laugh.**"

I had not the slightest idea where I was headed, but I said by faith, "I'll make a deal with you. If you will answer my question, then I will answer yours." He responded, "fair enough, what is your question"?

I knew at that point I had absolutely no answer to his question, and did not know what I would say after he answered my question. I then asked him the question the Holy Ghost had given me, **"what makes you laugh?"**

He cleared his throat, changed the tone of his voice like a professor about to give a profound lecture, looked down his nose at me, and said, "well that ought to be easy enough to answer." I sensed tenseness in the crowd. His face began to show signs of unexpected pressure, and I fully believe an obvious anointing had come upon me that he had never encountered. It was almost like

David and Goliath. I sensed a little taste of what David must have felt as he was forced into total dependence upon God.

He began an eloquent discourse on laughter, changing the tone and sound of his voice to that of an orator. In a deeper, Shakespearian voice he said, "you see, when God created man, he gave him an intellect, and an almost spiritual perception to comprehend words, ideas, situations, and experiences in communication with others that are ironic, coincidental, unique, or contains special factors of witticism and humor."

He continued, "God also gave man the intelligent ability to communicate in words, or spoken language. And, besides this he gave us another form of communication known as crying and laughter. Each serves a useful purpose of expressing sorrow or joy, or the conveying to another that we have caught the witticism of their pun, or joke, or ironic situation that is so coincidental that it is funny, or we have perceived their sorrow. When these things occur, laughter or crying are a normal, human, emotional response to a natural impulse through intellectual perception."

Just as he was finishing his speech, it was obvious that he was becoming aware that he was setting himself up for an indefensible rebuttal.

I responded, "Exactly! And, when God created me he placed in me a spiritual ability to respond to the divine impulse of his presence and anointing through praise, worship, adoration, exuberant joy, and even sometimes shouting and cheering similar to rejoicing at a ball game over a touchdown by the hometown team."

I continued, using almost his exact explanation, "shouting is a normal, human, emotional response to a divine impulse through spiritual perception. I do not deny that it is emotionalism in its best and most Biblical form. Just as a person can overdo even laughter, so have Pentecostals sometimes gone beyond the Spirit's expression and worship, and I cannot defend that, but there is such a thing as a purely Spiritual emotionalism expressed in genuine laughter, praise, joy, exuberance, worship, thanksgiving, hallelujahs and excitement and genuine pleasure in these ways that believers can respond to God's presence, and their awareness of his divine word, and gratitude for his grace, goodness, kindness, mercy, forgiveness, and saving power ... that is better than making a touchdown ... and should be equally enjoyed and celebrated in a purely human and emotional way ... but definitely as a response to a divine impulse not feigned or worked up by the one rejoicing in and by the Spirit."

There was a loud silence. He was taken aback by my answer and before he could recover, the crowd began to heckle him; "he's got you preacher; you let that little boy put you down; what have you got to say preacher"?

Clapping and cheering began, and got louder. The crowd began to disperse, slapping one another on the back and laughing at the preacher who had lost. Some came and shook my hand expressing their amazement at my ability to hang in there. Some said they were going to come hear me preach sometime. It was obvious that some were of a different denomination, and were delighted to see Goliath fall. While some were not yet ready for "Pentecost," they knew they had heard a truth.

One thing is for sure, they did not know how my head was whirling and how my heart was beating out of my chest. I had been involved in real spiritual warfare far beyond anything I had ever experienced. The crowd had obviously forgotten about his first question concerning "tongues as the initial evidence" where I had lost, and lost big. But, I did not forget it. There was a little more to this encounter.

It seemed obvious that the Holy Ghost had completely discomfited the non-Pentecostal preacher, and he was unable to regain his composure. In fact, he became visibly upset at the jeering of the crowd, and when he did try to talk, they prevented him by their jesting and poking fun at him.

I'll believe it my way

He finally turned to me and said, "I have got to go, but come see me at my office sometime, and maybe I can help you get things straight. As he turned to walk away I said, "Well, you believe it your way and I'll believe it mine, and we'll both hope to make it to heaven." He agreed with a nod.

I did not realize that I was parroting something else that I had heard all my life and it even seemed to make sense. But, the Holy Ghost stopped me in my tracks and said, "Wait a minute! No you don't! You have no right to believe it <u>your</u> way, and that man believes it <u>his</u> way." He then brought the following scripture to my mind:

- *2PE 1:20 Knowing this first, that no prophecy of the scripture is of any private interpretation.*
  21 For the prophecy came not in old time by the will of man: but holy men of God spake as they were moved by the Holy Ghost.

No private interpretation

The Holy Ghost continued, "You have no right to your private interpretation, and that man to his. You both had better believe it God's way. Don't ever say that again to anybody, because it is not truth."

I left that place with an intense desire to study to show myself approved unto God, a workman that needeth not to be ashamed, rightly dividing the word of truth (2TI 2:15).

10

Contemporary Experiences

Leroy Butler

A remarkable event occurred when a dear friend of mine and I would go to a black neighborhood on the north side of our town. We would arrive early on Sunday mornings, before time to go to our church. We would go to the center of a black business neighborhood which had a couple of grocery stores, a restaurant, with a bar which had been filled until near dawn, and a barber shop which was the center of activity for several men who got out at an early hour.

On this occasion we first went into the barber shop, which we had done several times. I played my accordion and sang, and Leroy preached a short message. He had a remarkable ability to stir people into attention about heaven and divine judgment. It was not uncommon for the Holy Spirit to convict men on the spot, unexpectedly, and sometimes against their will ... but the power of God was strong, and sometimes some prayed fervently.

Next, we went across the street to the restaurant which was a sort of night club where we found numerous couples sitting in booths and at tables ... sleeping off hangovers. A tired little lady looked through a serving window at us. Leroy asked her if it was

OK for us to sing and preach to her customers. I suppose she was waiting for them to awaken so she could serve them breakfast, hoping to make a little money.

It was obvious by the way they were zonked out that they had partied all night, and I had little hope of arousing any interest among these near-dead folk. But Leroy, the most indomitable man I have ever known, said, "Brother, start playing your accordion and sing *Peace In The Valley.*"

When I began, it was hilarious as Leroy went around and began to shake them, telling them to wake up ... that we were going to have church. They were so limber and lifeless, try as they might, most of them just could not make it, but would flop down again like a rag doll. Leroy gave me swirling hand signals to come on out with the singing ... louder and louder. I responded and he kept going back, and around, until he had most of them sitting up and getting their eyes open a little. They all had such a hang-over, this was no easy task.

When they got awake enough to realize where they were, they began to look at each other in total disbelief. Leroy began to instruct them to look at me and listen to the words I was singing. He assured them that Jesus was coming, and they would be left behind if they did not pay attention. They tried their best, but sleepily, at best.

Leroy then asked me to sing, "It is no Secret What God Can Do." This song seemed to turn him on, and he took on an evangelistic fervor as though, if he did not get all these people saved, their blood might be on his hands. It was not long before he had every single person on their knees crying out to God for mercy. Several of them were there with someone who was not their marriage partner. It was a miracle how conviction gripped those people, and needless to say, I was singing under an anointing that I would have thought impossible at 7:45 A.M. Tears were flooding down my cheeks as I went from song to song, rejoicing as much as I was singing.

Finally, Leroy said to them, "you have been here committing sin against each other, against your husbands and wives, against your children, and against God. Now you leave this place and don't come back." Leroy knew the woman at the window might not like what he had said, and he turned to face her. Tears were running down her face, and she said, "that is OK. I hope they all get saved, and you all come back anytime you want."

Everyone got up with tears in their eyes, hugging us, shaking our hands, as they began going out the door. As the last woman started out the door, the power of the Spirit came upon Leroy and he stopped her as she stood against the half-opened screen door. He asked, "Sister, do you know anything about the Holy Ghost?" She replied, "no sir, I have never gone to church and I don't know anything at all about that stuff."

Leroy said to me, "Brother, let's lay hands on this woman. God wants to baptize her in the Holy Ghost." You can understand my amazement when we simply laid hands on her, and her hands flew into the air while she began to speak in a language which sounded perfectly foreign. This continued for several minutes. She actually did not know what had happened to her, but she knew it was divine. She had been sovereignly filled with the Holy Ghost just like those at Pentecost, at Cornelius' house, and at Ephesus.

We explained what had happened, wrote some scripture locations for her to read, and sent her away rejoicing. As she went across the street, through a vacant lot, and disappeared between some buildings, she was waving her hands to God and rejoicing for her new-found fellowship with God. I wished we could follow up more, but that was not possible at the time. We encouraged her to find some new friends who knew about Jesus and the Holy Ghost, and left her in God's hands … and commended her to God … much like Paul did at Ephesus:

- *ACT 20:25 And now, behold, I know that ye all, among whom I have gone preaching the kingdom of God, shall see my face no more.*
  32 ***And now, brethren, <u>I commend you to God, and to the word of his grace</u>, which is able to build you up, and to give you an inheritance among all them which are sanctified.***

B. H. Clendennen

An interesting incident was related by Brother B.H. Clendennen, from Beaumont, Texas. He had the opportunity to minister in South Viet Nam, during the war. It was a miracle that he was allowed to go into secured governmental and military facilities which were highly restricted. It was his opportunity to speak to people who knew only about the religion of the Vietnamese, plus a few who had limited knowledge regarding Christianity. But, before the meeting he was warned that he could say nothing about the Holy Spirit in the Pentecostal sense. It would be permissible to make reference to the Holy Spirit, but not the baptism in the Holy Ghost. The religious leaders in charge said this would introduce confusion, and informed him that if he did so, there would be secret agents in the audience who would escort him out.

The night before the meeting, he was tempted to decline, rather than submit to such a limitation. He and his wife prayed in their hotel room for guidance, and he concluded that he had wondered at times if a lot of Pentecostalism, and particularly speaking in tongues was not a learned or programmed response. He concluded that he would do just as they asked. He would magnify Christ, and make references to the Holy Spirit in the context of his present-day work as the messenger of Christ, while doing the work of Christ today through those who have received Christ.

He gave an invitation for those who wanted to be a person through whom Christ worked, but he said nothing about the gifts of the Spirit, especially speaking in other tongues.

I heard Brother Clendennen's wife relate the story, and how it changed her life to witness fifty-some people come forward. Brother Clendennen knew that the moment of truth had come. Could it be possible that these people who had come to make a commitment to Christ could be baptized in the Holy Ghost as sovereignly as on the day of Pentecost? Could they, or would they begin speaking in other tongues, just as spontaneously, without any knowledge of the phenomenon beforehand?

Suddenly, confusion began breaking out. It was evident that secret servicemen began to rise, but not knowing what to do. The interpreter turned to Brother Clendennen saying, "something is wrong ... these people are acting strangely ... they may be losing their minds." Brother Clendennen asked, "what's the problem?" It was obvious that they were all overwhelmed in ecstatic praise and worship, and Brother Clendennen suspected what had happened, but he asked again, "what's taking place?" The interpreter said, they are all talking, but not in their language. They are confused.

Every person in the line was sovereignly baptized in the Holy Ghost and began to speak in other tongues as the Spirit gave them utterance. There was no way Brother Clendennen could be blamed for it, nor held responsible for it ... neither could he take credit. God did it. I have relayed this story from memory, after several years have passed, but I am sure a copy of the complete story could be obtained from Brother Clendennen, of Beaumont, Texas.

Vessie Hargrave

There are continuous testimonies from somewhere in the world that speaking in other tongues is confirmed as being a supernatural utterance of a known language by someone who does not know the language at all. Vessie Hargrave was a man who gave his life to ministering in remote, mountainous jungles of Mexico. He was the first Caucasian they had ever seen. The son of American missionaries, he had been born in Mexico. He obtained his Doctorate from Trinity University in San Antonio, Texas. Having learned the language of Mexico as a child, he was very fluent in both English and Spanish which were both studied as part of his Doctoral Degree.

Early in adulthood he also ministered in Mexico. His desire was to reach tribes of people so far back in the mountains that they had never been contacted with the gospel of Christ. He pioneered such a successful work among the Mexican Indians that crowds of several thousand walked many miles to attend an annual conference. As the work grew, others from America traveled with him to the meetings. He told me personally that, on several occasions, he had heard native Mexicans speak beautiful English when they were filled with the Holy Ghost.

I personally heard Lee Watson, a very prosperous businessman from Atlanta, Georgia, as he spoke at a missionary convention in Memphis, Tennessee attended by several thousand people. He gave a report on a trip he had taken with Vessie Hargrave. Mr. Watson said they traveled into the mountains as far as possible by truck then transferred to a Jeep because the road became so rocky and impassable by other vehicles. Finally, they changed to donkeys and traveled for many more steep miles and came to a remote tribal mountain village.

Vessie had been ministering to these people for a few years, and was the only white man, or American, they had ever seen before Lee Watson and a few others who came. These people had experienced a mighty move of God, and many miracles like those in the Bible had occurred in their midst. Blindness, deaf ears, crooked limbs, deadly diseases, etc., had been healed. Demons had been cast out of many, and the dead had been raised.

Many of these small statured, barefooted people had walked for days, bringing their sick, lame, and demented for help. This was a special, annual meeting attended by several thousand natives. The crowd pressed right against the two white men as they began to pray and minister to the people's needs.

Suddenly a woman in the crowd began to speak quite loudly in beautiful, unbroken English, with no dialect ... perfect English. She sounded like an ordinary, everyday American.

Lee Watson said he looked with startled amazement to Vessie Hargrave, and said, "I did not know there were any Americans here, or anyone who could speak English. Vessie replied, "there isn't." She has just received the baptism in the Holy Ghost. The woman who was obviously an uneducated Mexican Inca Indian continued for a long while in English, praising God and magnifying Jesus as Lord, Savior, Redeemer, and coming King. These are reputable men, and I heard the testimony from them personally.

O. E. and Betty Waters

A long-time acquaintance and dear Christian brother and wife, O.E. and Betty Waters, who live in my hometown, felt a call to minister in Mexico, so they bought a passenger bus and had it converted to a motor home. They began to make frequent trips into Mexico taking food, clothing, Bibles and medical supplies.

They were at an age when normally they would be thinking of retirement, but here they were, keeping themselves exhaustingly busy. They were not sponsored by any organization, and did the entire ministry on their own. A few people would help them gather clothing and other items for Mexico, and some would give donations of money, but by-and-large, most of the items and money would come from their own pockets and self-efforts. O. E. operated a successful used Automobile business.

Eventually, their married children, other relatives, close friends, and even church associates and ministers began to discourage them from making another grueling trip to Mexico. They were also placed in grave physical danger at times. Their friend's reasons for why they should not go were realistic and their arguments persuasive, but, O.E. and Betty just could not be talked out of it.

Some of the church people became almost offensive as they began to tell them they were not authorized to do missionary work, since they were not officially approved by the mission board of some church. This hurt, but they kept smiling and went on anyway, believing they were called of God to this work. Needless to say, Satan used this to his advantage because some had even slacked off from being supportive financially.

They found themselves asking God if they were in his will, and nagging doubts began to arise. They had just about decided to make their last trip when God gave them a miracle.

They had gone to a little country church deep into Mexico to help an aged lady missionary who had been there many years. She had started two churches, and they had finished service in one and were on their way to the other church. They followed the lady missionary who was driving her car ahead of the bus. Suddenly her car's engine stopped, and her efforts to restart the engine failed.

Finally, when O.E. tried to start her car, it started immediately, and he thought this was a little strange. He offered to drive the missionary's car the rest of the way, just in case it acted up again.

Betty Waters was accustomed to driving the bus, so the missionary lady rode with her as they continued their trip.

There were several young Mexican men in the missionary's car with O. E. In their excitement over the car running again, they began to worship and sing as they went down the road. Their worship turned into praise and it seemed to O.E. that some were beginning to praise in other tongues, since it did not sound like they were speaking Spanish which was the only language they knew.

Suddenly, the one sitting next to O.E. turned to him, and began to speak in perfect English. He began to tell O.E. about those who had tried to discourage him from coming to Mexico, but assured him that he was in God's perfect will. He was told not to listen to men, but trust in God.

We can imagine O.E.'s reaction of amazement when something so supernatural like that happened. The truth is, it actually did occur. There was no doubt in O.E.'s mind that God had spoken to him directly and personally through that uneducated Mexican youth. It confirmed many things to O.E., one of which was the validity of speaking in other tongues as being literal human languages. O.E. and Betty wept as they related the story to me and my wife, Margaret.

Thomas Ball Barratt

Thomas Ball Barratt who had founded the famous Filadelfia Church in Oslo, Norway, visited the Azusa Street Mission in 1905, and received the message concerning the Holy Spirit which was being poured out abundantly. He returned home and became known as the Father of the Pentecostal Movement in Europe. He also spent a year in India, during which time illiterate Indian girls who knew no English prayed and praised the Lord in Perfect

English. The same thing happened in China among ignorant Chinese who knew no English.

(Ref. "Warning! Do Not Seek for Tongues," Page 118, By Joe E. Campbell, Th.D.)

C. B. and Lorell Anderson

I co-pastored for thirteen years with C.B. Anderson, and his wife, Lorell, who had been missionaries to India for seventeen years. I asked them if they had ever heard native Indians speak in English while they were speaking in tongues. They said they had heard this happen several times.

My personal experience

When I was seventeen years of age, I experienced speaking in tongues for the first time while attending a rural church in Mount Olive, Tennessee. Immediately thereafter, I was bombarded with doubts concerning the experience. Prior to experiencing speaking in other tongues, I had resolved in my mind that, if I ever spoke in tongues, it would be the real thing ... and not done by me. I guarded against being prompted by such a strong desire that I would help the Holy Ghost a little. Nevertheless, after it happened, I was still challenged by Satan who accused me of being over-anxious.

It happened as follows: I had gone forward to the altar in response to an invitation. A couple of dear farmers who were real prayer-warriors knelt with me and began to encourage me to submit to the Holy Ghost and let him baptize me. I had come to the altar just to pray ... not to get involved in seeking for the infilling of the Holy Ghost ... but they were persistent. I began to feel guilty for my lack of motivation, and through a prayer of confession for this attitude, I sensed a deep, warm, loving presence of God overtake my spirit in a special way.

As I had done many times before, I began intently seeking to be filled. Of course, I expectantly wanted to speak in other tongues, but was at a total loss as to how to submit, or allow the Holy Spirit to baptize me. Several things these men said helped me greatly. I knew they were rough, hard-working, sincere men who loved God with all their heart. Their diamond-hard qualities and value would not be recognized by most churchmen, or ministries, but I recognized that God knew them, and they were anointed to pray with me.

One said to me, "son, don't pray with your lips, pray with your heart." That struck home, and immediately I began to sense my prayer, and praises coming from my innermost being. I began to wait until genuine, heart-felt praises would spring forth like a geyser. In a few moments I felt a praise begin to surge forth like a soft, moving rumble, deep in my spirit, and I just held back, suppressing it a little.

Tears of joy and praise filled my dry eyes, gushing forth like tiny flowing streams tracing their way down my cheeks. The hot tears flowed over my lips and splashed onto the altar below my face.

At this point, I must relate that one dear brother must have loved garlic and onions. While he was helping me, the devil was using his garlic breath to hinder me. I backed away, and finally put my face down beside the altar to get away from his ever-increasing "hallelujahs" and "amens."

My legs began to hurt from kneeling for so long, and as I attempted to change positions to sitting sideways, somehow I turned a little too far, and wound up in a painfully twisted position, hanging onto the heavy wooden altar bench for support. In desperation I turned the altar loose and could not keep from going flat on my back alongside the altar. The dear farmer could now reach right over the altar with his face right above mine. I thought I could not take this, but the spirit of prayer, worship, and praise was on me so mightily that I was more interested in keeping the momentum of the spiritual flow; therefore, I slid my face right under the bench-type altar and kept praising God with great joy.

I reached the point that my praise was no longer a mental or intellectual effort, and I would wait upon the words to come from the depths of my innermost being. I had the sensation of a spontaneous, free-flowing artesian well swelling up from within, and I just waited. I could hold it back no longer, and the word "hallelujah" came slowly rolling out in a deep, crying, rejoicing expression of praise.

But, I got only a couple of syllables out when the last two did not fit the word. My mind suddenly reasoned that I had become so ecstatic in praise that I had got mixed up, so I thought about that a few seconds when, here came that deep, wonderful feeling of praise again. I determined that I would take care not to help the Holy Ghost, meticulously avoiding going into gibberish, or non-intelligible utterances on my own, to avoid thinking I was speaking in other tongues when I was not.

But the same thing happened again, even with my trying to say "hallelujah" carefully and precisely. Those last two syllables came again, exactly as the first time. The inner-explosion of praise became stronger and my ability to hold it back became less as the urge came in the form of the words "glory to God."

Needless to say, it was as though an involuntary speech force would finish my words, superimposing its will over mine, causing me to say sounds that did not come from me at all -- not my mind, or my will -- and yet it soon became obvious as I continued from various words and phrases, that my heart was sensing the very close presence of God.

I began to wonder why this was coming forth, half English, and half something else. Once again God used one of the farmers who said, "the devil is a tricky old fellow. He will take advantage of you through your honesty and sincerity. He will try to convince you that it is you getting your tongue tangled up right while the Holy Ghost is helping you turn your speaking over to him."

I thought that over a little, and, hey! I felt that deep moving of the Spirit in my soul again and I determined I would not try to hold back. I relaxed and the praises began to flow, but not in my language, but quite soon I began to take back over with my sincere logical reasoning ... "It will not be me when I speak in tongues."

Then the devil began to whisper in my ear, "that cannot be God ... there was such a little of it." About that time God used one of the farmers again, who said, "Accept by faith whatever God gives you. If he gives you a spoonful, accept it. Don't refuse it because it is not a shovelful. God has more, and if you do accept the spoonful, it will be easy to believe for the shovelful. Don't worry! God has a tubful."

I suddenly realized that I must accept by faith what God had given, and even if it was seemingly a small quantity, that was not what mattered. It was the substance that was important. I found myself momentarily believing that I had spoken in tongues, at least a little.

Once I began to accept this gift of God by faith, I found it easier to shove Satan's suggestions and doubts into the background. The Holy Ghost truly took control, and it was almost like listening to someone else speak through my vocal cords. The sounds began to take the form of a foreign language, and by an utterance that came from within without any prompting from my mind or intellect, I worshipped and praise God for several minutes. I was refreshed, relaxed, overcome with joy and felt pleasant inner peace ... and I was satisfied that I had truly spoken in other tongues as the Spirit gave the utterance.

But, as I said, on the way home, the devil jumped on me with all four feet. My rational mind began to convince me that I had, after all, maneuvered myself into an emotional release to satisfy a spiritual longing. Several days of frustration followed, and I hardly had the spirit to pray, let alone expect to speak in tongues again.

At that time I was a student at Lee College in Cleveland, Tennessee, where, a week later I had another outstanding encounter with the Holy Ghost.

Following a student assembly and chapel service, a few students lingered in the main auditorium. They began to talk about God and started praying. I was so miserable, confused, and unsure of my experience that I said, "God, I am going backstage and get between those heavy velvet curtains and stay there until I settle this issue. Either I received the Holy Ghost and spoke in other tongues, or I did not. I have got to know, and I will settle this issue, or stay there until my bones bleach." I knew no one would know I was there, and it would be several days before the auditorium would be used again. The huge backdrop curtains were spaced about two feet apart and would give me an excellent place to hide away with God.

I slipped around through a side door, making sure no one saw me. I knelt and began to explain my plight to God. Almost before I could get started, that well of water began to flow, first like an artesian spring, then like a fountain, then like a geyser -- splashing, gushing, overflowing, lifting high in praise, then subsiding in soft worship. Ecstatic rapid words would rush forth in utterances unfruitful to my understanding. Then slow, rolling words filled with emotions of sheer worship and adoration would swell forth.

Then praises in English would lavish the Holy One, yet in eloquence and expressions that were beyond me in literary style and excellence, comparable to Shakespearean quality. I knew that God was showing me that the Holy Ghost was able, not only to speak in other languages through me, but he was able to speak through my own language, yet under his control, and not mine. This went on for several minutes and I was totally satisfied and convinced, because all doubt had been removed, and remains removed to this day. God had been gracious to me to give me such a convincing experience, and I loved him for it.

But, I had no idea what was about to happen next. I was surprised to find that the other students were still in the auditorium. Several thicknesses of heavy velvet curtains had made the space around me practically soundproof. I sat down with the group who were singing some songs. We began to softly sing, "Search me, oh God, and know my heart today." It suddenly dawned on me that, without realizing it I had switched to singing in the Spirit … in other tongues.

Jean Suleiman

About that time, a foreign student named Jean Suleiman, said, "Listen! Mac is singing in French! I kept on singing … just submitting … not trying to keep on … but not trying to stop either … just singing, and worshipping to the depths of my soul.

I was not out in a trance, but fully conscious, sitting in a theatre-type auditorium seat. I had my eyes closed and my face looking upward. I could hear their discussion of what was happening. Jean began to interpret everything I was singing, and for several minutes I was spell-bound by what was coming out of my mouth. It was literally beautiful. Jean had the natural French accent that can make English so beautiful. French was her native language.

The praise was all about Jesus … who he was … his involvement in creation … his relationship to the Father … his Godhead …

his mission to earth ... his glorious ministry, suffering, death, resurrection, ascension, his future reign as King-of-Kings and Lord-of-Lords over his Kingdom, and ... on and on. The phraseology was so far beyond me that it is unbelievable. Things came forth about his Kingdom that I did not even know, but learned later through study -- His heavenly Priesthood, his anticipated Millennial Kingship.

All those around me were softly weeping, praising, speaking in tongues, and listening at the same time, as they listened to the Spirit as he used me to bring forth supernatural anthems of praise that moved in and out of unbelievable poetry ... to prose ... in eloquent descriptive phrases and adjectives ... all conforming to the beautiful melody of the song, *"Cleans Me."* Jean understood every word in French and interpreted it all in English.

After the power and unction of the Spirit subsided within me, excited discussions began with all sorts of questions and answers. These students -- my friends -- knew me, and they knew I could not do that on my own. Jean Suleiman was disbelieving, and yet she had heard it for herself, in her own language. The others questioned her thoroughly. They questioned me: What was it like? How did you feel? Were you in a trance? Could you hear us? Could you hear Jean as she told us what you were saying? What were you thinking? Did the thoughts come and then you sing them? Were you thinking in English as you were singing in tongues? Was it hard to keep going for so long? Were there any momentary hesitations in your mind? Was God speaking to you? Did it feel good?

I recall the experience as vividly as if it were yesterday. I remember the inner peace and pleasure I experienced as I listened to the obviously French sounding vowels and consonants formed involuntarily. I knew there had to be a supernatural source for what I was doing because there was no way under the sun that I could even pretend to speak in French and make it sound like the language. It was obvious that I was actually singing in a foreign language the same way as on the day of Pentecost.

I will never forget when I looked straight into the eyes of Jean and asked her intently, "Jean, are you sure?" She looked back at me with even deeper intensity as she replied, "If you heard someone speak in English, wouldn't you be sure?"

We all knew that we were not lying to each other. This was real. This was Biblical. Something had happened to us that would never be taken out of our hearts. Faith in Jesus as the baptizer in the Holy Ghost was confirmed beyond any doubt. Resolve broke into fervent flames within all of us as we determined to find those who were being robbed of this miraculous truth and help them to understand the reality and importance of this beautiful and marvelous gift ... which was clearly outlined in everyone's Bible.

We suddenly understood why Satan would fight it so hard. We had tasted; we had felt; we had seen! And, Satan does not want that. He does not want us to experience the real, true, authentic, spiritual power of God. He works through neighbors, friends, relatives, and even preachers, to prevent anyone from moving into the realm of the Spirit to this extent.

Everyone has the power to choose what they want to believe. One must choose to believe the Bible just as it is without limiting the truth of God's word contained therein. God can, and will confirm his word to those who hunger and thirst after righteousness.

- *MAT 5:6 Blessed are they which do hunger and thirst after righteousness: for they shall be filled.*
- *MAR 16:20 And they went forth, and preached everywhere, the Lord working with them, and confirming the word with signs following.*

- *ACT 5:32 And we are his witnesses of these things; and so is also the Holy Ghost, whom God hath given to them that obey him.*

Paul and Delores Blissett

I led a Bible Study in the home of the Blissetts for several months. We would close each session with prayer. Usually we would form a circle and various ones would pray as they felt led. Normally I allowed others to pray, but on occasion I chose to pray the dismissal prayer, and while doing so I began to pray in tongues, and when I finished Paul said, "Mac, you prayed in perfect Spanish."

Paul and Delores had been directors of a Bible College in Mexico for many years, and they both spoke Spanish fluently. Paul was a very honest and humble man who would not have said such a thing before his wife if it were not true.

A few weeks later at the close of another meeting the same thing happened again. Naturally, I was thankful to God for the experience. Since I was planning to write this book, it bolstered my faith and confidence that I was pursuing a course that pleased God and hopefully would bless others.

Needless to say, I firmly believe that God has anointed me heavily at times while writing these things which I believe are taken straight from the word of God.

Jack Smith, Oakwood, Texas

An amazing encounter with the Holy Ghost was experienced by Jack Smith, Sr., who lived in Oakwood, Texas. Jack had been appointed as the Sunday School Superintendent of a Baptist church in Oakwood. It was his duty to moderate the opening exercises of the Sunday School at the beginning of the Sunday Morning service. He made announcements and then gave a limited devotional before the assembly went to their various classrooms.

Jack took this responsibility seriously because he had a deep commitment regarding the spiritual care of the Lord's sheep that had been placed upon him. His daily life took on a deeper level of commitment to prayer, Bible reading, and guarding his thoughts, words and actions as he went about his daily activities.

His secular job was to drive a bull dozier clearing land of trees and brush, building dams for stock ponds, and preparing building sites. One morning he felt a strong urge to pray while he worked. There were other workers in the area, but he knew they could not hear him praying because of the noise of the bull dozier's diesel engine. Much to his own surprise, when he began to pray he began to cry, shedding a flood of tears. An overwhelming emotion of worship and praise to God came over him and the feeling was like divine electricity. His intention was to pray to God regarding his Sunday School superintending, but instead, his focus centered on God and what Jack was experiencing for the first time.

He said his praises became so loud that he shoved the throttle to full open, and let the praises flow. He knew he was not going to do anything to turn off this heavenly waterfall that was bathing his soul with ecstatic joy. He was crying aloud using every praise word he knew … words which had never been his common prayer vocabulary. Hallelujah, glory, praise God, thank you Jesus, amen, wonderful Lord, and my Savior, plus more seemed to roll off his tongue and out of his mouth fluently. This had never been his nature, or religious personality, and never had he experienced anything like it. This went on for a large part of the day.

The next day he was dumbfounded as he looked back on what had happened to him and he knew he had struck a vein of gold somewhere deep in his soul. It had felt so good he would be the last person to doubt the reality of what he had tasted from God.

As he started the engine of his machine he began to thank God for yesterday's blessing. When he got into full swing of roaring into trees and pushing them down he said, "God let it happen again." He put the throttle wide open because he felt another wave coming. Tears of joy gushed out of his eyes. A torrent of praise even more powerful lifted his soul into a realm of heavenly adoration of the great God he served, and that had become so close and personal to him.

In fact, as he bathed his God with floods of praise, the words became jumbled and mixed as the rush of joy and adoration was faster than he could keep up. He finally could not even say the words, the spiritual current was flowing too fast, and he was being swept along with the tide. He reached a point where all he could do was jabber and attempt to speak intelligently, but he was so enraptured with the divine presence that had engulfed him, he quit trying to say his own words, and enjoyed the moment without understanding why such was happening to him.

Well, this went on for a few days more, and then came Sunday Morning. When it was time for his devotional he decided to tell the people what had happened to him. He told how he had started to pray to God asking for his help and guidance regarding his duty as Sunday School superintendent. He went into detail describing how he had been so overcome by a spirit of praise and worship, and how it had happened repeatedly.

He then recommended that every one of them go out into the woods and pray to God while hoping the same thing would happen to them. At that moment the pastor stepped in and stopped him. He told the people to ignore what they had just heard. He turned to Jack Smith and told him, "You are not going to make

Pentecostals out of us. This is a Baptist church and we do not speak in tongues here."

Jack was dumbfounded because he knew absolutely nothing about the Holy Ghost or speaking in tongues. He told the pastor he did not know what he was talking about, but his words fell on deaf ears.

The pastor announced that the service was dismissed, and they were all to go home, which they did. When they returned for their regular Sunday evening service, the pastor had put a hasp and a padlock on the door with a sign informing them the church was closed until further notice.

Upon seeing the locked door, the whole crowd proceeded to Jack Smith's door and they filled his house to overflowing. There were a few people there that knew more about the Holy Ghost than Jack did. They began a diligent search to see what information they could find in the Bible on the subject, and to make a long story short, Jack was enlightened from the Bible regarding what had happened to him, and most of the church became also convinced and experienced a mighty outpouring of the Holy Spirit.

This has grown into a dynamic local church where many people have been enlightened regarding the infilling of the Holy Spirit. I was privileged to participate in the early days of this move of God, I preached numerous times, and even held a revival where gifts of the spirit were manifested in undeniable and infallible proofs.

I was privileged to be one of the speakers for several annual conventions sponsored by the church. Acquaintance with the church and area-wide fellowship among surrounding churches developed.

A New Song

I was invited to minister during a weekend of special services. While I was driving to Oakwood, I began to sing a song which I had recently written. I had received the song while reading where Peter said to the lame man at the gate of the temple, "silver and gold have I none, but such as I have give I to thee." Peter then took him by the hand and told him to stand up. The lame man was instantly healed.

- *ACT 3:4 And Peter, fastening his eyes upon him with John, said, Look on us.*
  5 And he gave heed unto them, expecting to receive something of them.
  6 Then Peter said, Silver and gold have I none; but such as I have give I thee: In the name of Jesus Christ of Nazareth rise up and walk.
  7 And he took him by the right hand, and lifted him up: and immediately his feet and ancle bones received strength.
  8 And he leaping up stood, and walked, and entered with them into the temple, walking, and leaping, and praising God.
  9 And all the people saw him walking and praising God:

The words to the song are as follows:

SUCH AS I HAVE

Verse 1
The beggar so low, deep in despair
Sat by the gate with no one to care.
He looked with delight when Peter stooped low,
Only to say, "No silver or gold."

Verse 2
The beggar I know could have been me
Lost and alone, deeply in need,
When Jesus bent low and lifted me up
What silver and gold he placed in my cup.

Verse 3
No silver or gold I hold in my hand,
But treasures untold I command.
My Father owns all on a thousand hills;
He left it to me, It's all in the Will.

Chorus
Such as I have, give I to thee,
Such as I have, t'was given to me,
Freely received, freely to give,
In Jesus' name, stand up and live!

I intended to sing the song that evening before I preached. I felt that God had assured me that he would bless the song as I sang it as a means to bless his people. When I ended the song with the last phrase, *"In Jesus name, stand up and live,"* the whole congregation leaped to their feet and began to praise God.

It was obvious that a mighty outpouring of the Holy Spirit was sweeping the place. It was reported that twelve people had spontaneously experienced the gift of speaking in tongues for the first time.

The pastor's wife, Dianne, testified that she had been suffering from a terrible migraine headache for three weeks, and had gone to three different doctors in an attempt to gain relief. She declared, mingled with excited praise, that when she leaped to her feet, the headache completely left.

There were a group of teenaged young men that came forward and kneeled at the front of the church. I later learned they had not accepted the Holy Spirit move which had overtaken their parents, and they were embarrassed among their friends, because it had created quite a stir throughout the community and especially among their friends at school. But, this night God spoke to them by the Holy Spirit and they came forward and repented. Needless to say, I did not get to preach that night because there was such joy in the camp over these sons who had kneeled at the foot of the cross.

Several times throughout the following weeks and months I called Jack and Dianne, and learned that the migraine headaches which had been a frequent problem had not returned. There were also other testimonies where God had miraculously given a divine touch of healing.

Supernatural dentistry

A lady in the church gave an amazing testimony. I do not recall if she was one who leaped to her feet when so many were touched, but soon thereafter she said she had gone to the dentist with a pounding tooth ache. He drilled out the decay and filled the cavity with a temporary filling because he doubted the tooth could be saved.

She returned to the dentist in a few days, and when he looked in her mouth he asked who had filled her tooth. She replied that she had not been to any dentist, but at church she had asked God to heal her tooth.

He told her that he had drilled out an irregular shaped cavity, but there was a perfectly round filling in a perfectly round cavity, and it looked like a pure silver filling. He took some more x-rays to compare to his file and sent her on her way rejoicing. The dentist acknowledged that it had to be a miracle.

A child healed of asthma

On a later date I went with Jack and Diane to a church a few miles away from Oakwood. I had been invited to preach, and in the middle of my message I noticed a commotion a few rows back. Since several were standing and obviously praying over a couple, I asked if there was a problem. The couple both stood up. The father was holding a baby boy which had leaned backwards over his arm. The mother said, I believe our baby has just died. She explained that he frequently had acute asthma attacks, and the doctor had described the case as being so severe that they could expect a fatal attack at any time. She said he had just suffered probably the worst attack ever, and had stopped breathing.

I could easily see the seriousness of the situation because the child was turning blue, his eyes were rolled back in his head, and he was totally limp on his father's arm. I told the church we were going to pray and ask God to bring the child back to life and heal him.

As we prayed the child raised up perfectly erect, looked around at his surroundings, as though he was wondering what was going on. His color returned to normal, and his father and mother hugged and embraced him as they both cried in amazement and disbelief.

I asked the parents if they knew Jesus as their Lord and Savior. They said they were only visitors to this church with some friends who had invited them. They explained they were Catholics and had never been in a church like this. It was so strange to them, but all their defenses were broken down because they had just witnessed a miracle. They were humble and willing to learn, and you can guess that I did not get to finish my sermon because the church was energized with praise as the parents were gloriously born again by the Holy Spirit as they confessed Christ as their Lord and Savior.

Afterwards, for several weeks later I called Dianne and Jack to check on the little boy, and they reported that he had no more asthma attacks.

I am telling these things to encourage anyone and everyone to believe in the Biblical truth regarding the Holy Spirit. One can know that if they will dare to believe what the Bible says, they will experience many amazing blessings. By taking the first few steps regarding the fruit of the Spirit, and by embracing the truth of the gifts of the Spirit, this will open heaven's door to the manifestation of all the gifts as they are revealed in the Bible.

My personal healing at Oakwood

From childhood I had suffered frequent sickness from what I learned was esophageal reflux disease. Sometimes I would have a sick spell almost weekly, and frequently twice a week. The attacks would be accompanied by severe headaches and, acidic regurgitation, and prolonged vomiting. I would be about as sick all over as one could get.

This continued throughout my life and resulted in many days of lost time. I carried on as best I could, in spite of the frequent attacks. I was careful to control my diet, took over-the-counter medicines of various kinds, but obtained little relief from the inevitable spells of sickness.

I was invited to be the morning speaker at an annual convention held by the Oakwood church. My wife and I stayed in a nearby motel. About two A.M. I awoke knowing an esophageal reflux attack was coming on strong. A splitting headache, upset stomach, and up-chucking ensued, and by daylight I could hardly hold my head up, and I was supposed to preach at 10:00 A.M.

"There was a restaurant associated with the motel. My wife encouraged me to try to eat something, and hopefully I might be able to hold something on my stomach. This I did, and slight relief came, but I was still very ill when I entered the pulpit. I persevered and delivered the message which I had received a few days earlier. To say the least, I was very perplexed concerning why I had not been healed. In fact, I had prayed for the healing of others while I was seriously ill.

On one occasion, I was preaching while enduring a severe headache, which I knew would lead into a severe bilious attack. A lady named Sister Suggs interrupted my preaching, and while coming forward toward me said, 'Brother Symes, I have got such a terrible migraine headache that I must leave if I am not healed.

I thought, who am I to be praying for her healing while I also have a debilitating headache? I was about to confess to her and to the church that I was not qualified to pray for her because of my own need for healing. I intended to call for some of the church folk to gather around her for prayer when the Lord spoke to me, clearly saying, **"Divine healing is not dependent upon the condition of your physical body, but on the stripes Jesus bore on his body for our healing."**

He brought to my mind the following scripture.

- *1PE 2:24 Who his own self bare our sins in his own body on the tree, that we, being dead to sins, should live unto righteousness:* ***by whose stripes ye were healed.***

With that word from God I anointed Sister Suggs with oil according to the scripture, and she was instantly healed, and so was I. But I was not permanently healed at that time. God had something else in mind.

Now, back to Oakwood. I made it through the 10:00 A.M. message, and went back to the motel bed. A young Pastor from Louisiana was to minister in the evening service. I very much wanted to attend, but was weak from the lingering effects of my sick spell. I went anyway, and at the conclusion of his message he invited anyone needing prayer to come forward. Over the years I had responded to almost every such invitation hoping my time would come for healing. In fact I had almost become discouraged from trying again, but I went anyway.

A line formed and I was the last in line. Almost every person ahead of me fell out when they were prayed for. This had become almost a spectacular phenomenon throughout the land as many would fall out and line the floor like cordwood. I was finding it hard to reconcile this with scriptural events recorded in the New Testament. In spite of this I was attempting to curb any critical spirit that might impede the flow of the Spirit, and most of all, I wanted to be healed.

I was willing to fall out if this is what God wanted, but I assured him that if I did fall, it would be by his power, and not by my help in any way. I knew there were scriptural instances where people fell under the power of God, and that is what I wanted, pure and simple.

When my time came, with people lying all around me, I stood erect, but mentally submissive to whatever God wanted. The minister placed his hands firmly on my head and began to move it around, forward and backward, side to side, and in a circular motion.

I am an instrument rated pilot, having owned my own aircraft, and in my instrument training the instructor had attempted to induce vertigo in my head while I was under the hood which kept me from seeing anything but the aircraft instrument panel. He did all sorts of dips and dives, spins and stalls, but to no avail. My vision was blocked by the hood and the only thing I could see was straight ahead at the instrument panel. He finally gave up and said I was very resistant to vertigo which was a good thing.

As the minister was moving my head around, I recalled that many people become dizzy from such gyrations of the head. I resisted any attempt to rationalize the situation and kept telling God that if he wanted me to go down, it would have to be him because I was not going to help him.

The preacher became more aggressive as he pushed my head to the side and bent me sideways until my head was around waist level. The strain on my spine became almost unbearable as it seemed the preacher intended for me to go down. I said, "God, what am I supposed to do?"

Suddenly, a surge of divine virtue flowed through my entire body. My head whipped out from under his hands, and I stood with my hands raised, as I began loudly praising God with an overflowing force of joy.

God spoke to me clearly saying, "I have healed you because you were willing to stand for a truth."

When I returned to my seat I told my wife that God had healed me of the reflux disease. The church had prepared a fabulous dinner for the noon meal, and served another meal for just the ministers and their wives after the evening service. I went into the dining hall and loaded my plate with everything I should not eat. My wife went along cautioning me with every big helping I took.

I assured her I had heard from God, but she was not convinced. She said, "We'll see." She had nursed me through my bouts of sickness for years and knew what the normal results of a big nighttime meal would be.

After the evening service we intended to make the ninety-minute drive home. She warned me that I would never make it without needing to stop on the way and lose all that I had eaten. She said, "you know what happens when you eat a big meal before going to bed.

All the way home she kept asking me how I was feeling, and I assured her I was doing fine with no sick feeling coming on. I made it without a problem. That night I awakened frequently during the night, surprised that my morning hours were not accompanied by a building headache.

That occurred over thirty years ago, and I have never had another esophageal reflux attack, accompanied by the painful headache, extreme nausea, and daylong hangover. God completely and thoroughly healed me.

My wife, Margaret said, "We'll see," and we did. God did it!!

I do not have time or space to relate all the many miracles God has performed over the years, and Oakwood is certainly a memorable highlight, but there are many, many more just as spectacular. I hope to attempt to record most of them all someday.

I have given the above testimonies to emphasize the truth regarding the gifts of the Spirit, and to encourage everyone to *"live in the Spirit,"* and to *"walk in the Spirit."*

- *GAL 5:25 If we live in the Spirit, let us also walk in the Spirit.*

Jack Smith Senior has graduated to Glory, and his Son, Jack Junior, and his wife, Tina, carry on pastoring a thriving and growing New Testament church. In the month of May, 2021, Jack Junior told me they were about three week away from completing a new auditorium that seats three hundred and fifty people. Oakwood is a small country town in the heart of East Texas."

Emphasis on the Holy Spirit

While the title of this book indicates it is "ABOUT THE HOLY SPIRIT," emphasis is placed on speaking with tongues, and is also about the Holy Spirit personally, stressing all the fruits of the Spirit and all the gifts of the Spirit.

Today, there are many who claim to have received the Holy Spirit when they were born again, but they are practically silent concerning the fruit of the Spirit, and the gifts of the Spirit, especially regarding speaking in other tongues.

It does not take a deep study of the word of God to discover that speaking in tongues is only the beginning of living and walking in the Spirit, but those who receive the truth regarding speaking in tongues find that, willingness to walk in truth discussed in this book leads to many open doors of spiritual power and knowledge, meaning all the *"administrations," "operations,"* and *"manifestations,"* of the Holy Spirit.

- *1CO 12:5 And there are differences of **administrations**, but the same Lord.*
  *6 And there are diversities of **operations**, but it is the same God which worketh all in all.*
  *7 But the **manifestation** of the Spirit is given to every man to profit withal.*

There is an obvious association and correlation between speaking in tongues and all the other gifts. Those who accept and manifest the gifts of the Spirit are mainly those persons who also embrace speaking in tongues which is listed among the other gifts of the Spirit. Endorsing the gift of tongues opens the door to all the spiritual gifts. Every Christian should be motivated to strongly desire spiritual gifts.

- ***1CO 14:1 Follow after charity, and desire spiritual gifts …***

Besides the oral gifts, namely speaking in tongues, interpretation of tongues, and prophesy, the other supernatural gifts are essential for a fully rounded life in the Spirit. All the gifts are listed as follows:

- *1CO 12:7 But the manifestation of the Spirit is given to every man to profit withal.*

*8 For to one is given by the Spirit **the word of wisdom**; to another **the word of knowledge** by the same Spirit;*

*9 To another **faith** by the same Spirit; to another **the gifts of healing** by the same Spirit;*

*10 To another **the working of miracles**; to another **prophecy**; to another **discerning of spirits**; to another **divers (various) kinds of tongues**; to another the **interpretation of tongues**:*

11 But all these worketh that one and the selfsame Spirit, dividing to every man severally as he will.

It is God's will that every believer should speak in tongues. Verse 10 says "*diverse kinds of tongues.*" "*Diverse*" means different kinds," or various kinds. Around the world there are thousands of different languages spoken, and the Holy Spirit has access to any one of these different languages to use when he manifests speaking in tongues.

Paul was discussing speaking in other tongues as a gift of the Holy Spirit when he said the following:

- *1CO 14:10 There are, it may be, so many kinds of voices in the world, and none of them is without signification.*

He was saying, "There are so many kinds of languages in the world, and none of them is without meaning." The apostle Paul strongly believed in speaking with other tongues.

- *1CO 14:39 Wherefore, brethren, covet to prophesy, **and forbid not to speak with tongues.***

Paul also said,

- *1CO 14:18 I thank my God, **I speak with tongues more than ye all:***

11

Jesus is the Baptizer

I was raised in Pentecostal circles where it was taught that a person could get saved and then receive the Holy Ghost thereafter. Converts usually went into a long session of days, weeks, months, and even years tarrying until they were endued with power from on high. Tarrying was considered normal since this is what happened with the disciples who tarried in Jerusalem for ten days prior to Pentecost, waiting to receive the Holy Ghost.

Chronic seekers

For many years I was of the persuasion which was traditional in Pentecostal circles, and expected as the norm, that tarrying might entail a long period of time.

In the nineteen-sixties I preached a revival meeting for a fairly large church where there were twenty-five people which had been seeking, or "tarrying," for the baptism in the Holy Ghost for several years ... ranging from two to twenty-five years.

At the time, I did not know Biblically to tell them they had already received the Holy Ghost ... when they were born again. With increased Biblical knowledge, today, I would tell them to accept their Holy Ghost baptism as a Biblical fact, and to expect to experience any, and all, of the gifts (manifestations) (1CO 12:7)) of the Spirit -- including speaking in other tongues. I have come to realize that it is much easier to experience speaking in other tongues if one believes by faith they received the Holy Ghost into their body-temple when they were saved … and it is 100% scripturally sound.

I became heavily burdened for these 25 seekers because I knew something had to be wrong. I knew that the early church tarried for ten days, but they were waiting, as Jesus had instructed, until the Holy Spirit came. On this occasion Jesus had told them the Holy Ghost would come shortly.

- *ACT 1:5 For John truly baptized with water; but ye shall be baptized with the Holy Ghost not many days hence.*

Jesus had told them to not depart from Jerusalem, but wait until the Holy Ghost came, therefore they tarried for ten days, and true to the prediction of Christ, the Holy Ghost came.

It is not logical that this should set a precedent today that tarrying should be an expected prolonged prelude to being filled with the Holy Ghost.

In the revival meeting I was leading, when the invitation was given on the first night, the group of chronic seekers responded immediately because they desperately wanted to receive the Holy Spirit. They kneeled at various places around the front of the church, and became the focus of attention as others came forward to give prayerful assistance and encouragement as they "tarried" for the infilling of the Holy Ghost.

They were seeking for the manifestation of the gift of tongues as the initial evidence which would confirm that they had been baptized with the Holy Ghost. After a while, they all gave up -- convinced that tonight was not the night -- but were reassured in their own minds that their fervency had been demonstrated, and that God would someday reward their diligence.

Before someone thinks I am being too critical, let me say that I am thankful for this much. Many have received the fullness of the Holy Ghost under such circumstances because God is merciful in spite of our lack of Biblical knowledge and wisdom. God has done the best he could under the circumstances. I received the Holy Ghost under such circumstances, and it was a valid experience, but I remember the unnecessary difficulty in receiving the gift of tongues because I believed that the Holy Ghost would come in only as I began to speak in tongues. I believed I must experience speaking in tongues as the initial evidence that the Holy Ghost had come in. My church peers would not allow me to believe the Holy Ghost dwelled in me prior to when I spoke in other tongues.

The next day the pastor of the church where I was leading the revival hesitantly and cautiously approached me, warning me that these people were "chronic seekers," and had about exhausted everybody in the church, as well as every evangelist that had come along. He advised me against letting them occupy too much of my time, which would prevent me from ministering to others -- especially new people -- who also had needs.

I became heavily burdened for these precious people who were having such a struggle with allowing the Holy Spirit to manifest his gift through them. I began to fast and pray while seeking God's anointing to empower me to help these people. They had become a problem to the church and the pastor. They were in total frustration and desperation ... wondering why they could not receive the Holy Ghost just like many others around them who had received. They could see it in the Bible, but were completely perplexed in their attempt to experience it.

JESUS IS THE BAPTIZER

After three days of fasting and seeking God, I asked him, "What can I do or say that will help them?" The answer came clearly, "teach them that **Jesus is the Baptizer**." This was opened to me in a dimension that I had not seen before. That evening I preached a message entitled, "Jesus - The Baptizer."

The scripture came to me where God had spoken to John the Baptist regarding Jesus.

- *JOH 1:32 And John bare record, saying, I saw the Spirit descending from heaven like a dove, and it abode upon him. 33 And I knew him not: but he that sent me to baptize with water, the same said unto me, Upon whom thou shalt see the Spirit descending, and remaining on him, **the same is he which baptizeth with the Holy Ghost.** 34 And I saw, and bare record that this is the Son of God.*

It is important to notice these words were spoken by God himself to John the Baptist concerning his Son, Jesus.

Jesus considered this phase of his ministry to be extremely urgent because God had assigned the responsibility to him, as the head of the church, to administer the sending of the Holy Ghost to dwell in the life and body of every person who was saved because they received Jesus as their Savior and Lord.

Jesus told his disciples it was extremely urgent (*expedient*) that he return back to the presence of his Father in heaven, because from there he and the Father would work together to send the Holy Ghost to believers on earth. Jesus called the Holy Ghost "the Comforter."

- *JOH 16:7 Nevertheless I tell you the truth; It is expedient for you that I go away: for if I go not away, the Comforter will not come unto you; but if I depart, I will send him unto you.*

Jesus was the "Comforter" that had been with them, but they were here told that another Comforter was being sent to them, which was the Holy Ghost.

- *JOH 14:25 These things have I spoken unto you, being yet present with you.*
  26 But <u>the Comforter, which is the Holy Ghost</u>, whom the Father will send in my name, he shall teach you all things, and bring all things to your remembrance, whatsoever I have said unto you.
- *JOH 14:15 If ye love me, keep my commandments.*
  16 And I will pray the Father, and he shall give you another Comforter, that he may abide with you for ever;
  17 Even the Spirit of truth; whom the world cannot receive, because it seeth him not, neither knoweth him: but ye know him; for he dwelleth with you, and shall be in you.

To the Chronic Seekers I explained how it was not necessary, nor Biblical that they should tarry for days, or weeks, months, or years. I suggested that they all had their own mental or psychological barriers that had been built up that prevented their believing and receiving.

Some of them felt that sooner-or-later the right preacher would come along to lay hands on them and the Holy Ghost would fall on them. Some had thought I might be the right one, and so they rushed forward the first night of the meeting.

Some expected to be so overpowered by a mighty rush, and surge of spiritual power that they would be practically slain in the Spirit. Others expected a quiet, soft, gentle breeze of the Spirit to blow through their soul, relaxing all their tensions while they sweetly and quietly began to speak in other tongues ... finally victorious after a long, hard battle for submission. Others said they truly expected to be baptized in the quietness of their own home.

Do not seek for speaking in tongues

I had concluded that they were all seeking for the evidence of speaking in tongues more than seeking for the person of the Holy Spirit. They were more conscious of the utterances coming out of their mouth, than the praise that was coming from their heart. They were not aware of the presence of the Holy Spirit in their heart ... and of his dwelling in their bodies as his temple.

With strong emphasis, I explained why they should seek for the indwelling of the Holy Spirit because of who he is, and because of the fruit of the Spirit – "love, joy, peace, longsuffering, gentleness, goodness, faith, meekness, temperance" -- and for the gifts of the Spirit – "the word of wisdom, the word of knowledge, faith, the gifts of healing, the working of miracles, prophecy, discerning of spirits, divers kinds of tongues, the interpretation of tongues" -- which he gives to those who receive him ... in whom he takes up his abode.

They were then encouraged to focus their attention on the scriptures which magnify Christ as the one who baptizes in the Holy Ghost, realizing that when men laid hands on others, it was only symbolic of Christ's hands. One must look to Jesus only, as the author and finisher of their faith. One must not pre-conceive how they will be baptized, or how they will begin speaking in other tongues. One must rest in praises of Jesus while appreciating all the reasons for which the Holy Ghost was given to the church. One must not praise, just for the sake of praising, but must praise "for something."

They were encouraged to practice the reality of Jesus, believing and conceiving of him as very present ... and being there to help them yield and submit their whole being -- their body -- as vessels to contain the precious oil ... the gift of the Spirit.

- *1CO 6:19 What? know ye not that your body is the temple of the Holy Ghost which is in you, which ye have of God, and ye are not your own?*
  20 For ye are bought with a price: therefore glorify God in your body, and in your spirit, which are God's.
- *2CO 4:7 But we have this treasure in earthen vessels, that the excellency of the power may be of God, and not of us.*

With this teaching fresh in their spirits, all "chronic seekers" came forward, along with several who were newly converted, but had followed in the old tradition of first getting saved, then at a later time tarrying for the baptism of the Spirit. I reminded them that the Bible says at the time the Holy Ghost was poured out, the disciples were in one accord with each other. They were encouraged to embrace a spirit of unity and love toward their brethren.

- *ACT 2:1 And when the day of Pentecost was fully come, they were all with one accord in one place.*

Also, it was shown how the disciples were praising and magnifying God when the Holy Ghost fell upon them.

- *LUK 24:51 And it came to pass, while he blessed them, he was parted from them, and carried up into heaven.*

52 And they worshipped him, and returned to Jerusalem with great joy:
53 And were continually in the temple, <u>praising and blessing God</u>.

The Holy Ghost Fell

What happened that night, and for the next two nights was phenomenal. As these "chronic seekers" forgot about everything but Jesus, it began to be easy for them to believe in Jesus as the Baptizer ... that he would help them walk in the power of the Holy Spirit. One-by-one they began to receive the manifestation of the gift of tongues, by which they glorified and magnified the Lord. In addition, most began to speak boldly in English as well -- interspersed with speaking in other languages -- telling the church of the greatness of God. It was truly a dual manifestation of prophetic utterance by the Holy Ghost ... part in their own language and part in tongues (languages) unknown to them. The supernatural anointing upon them was very obvious ... without doubt, as obvious as what Simon the sorcerer saw when the Holy Ghost was poured out at Samaria, or as obvious as when the Holy Ghost fell on the men at Ephesus.

- *ACT 19:6 And when Paul had laid his hands upon them, the Holy Ghost came on them; and they spake with tongues, and prophesied.*
  7 And all the men were about twelve.

In helping these people, I had drawn from some of my own struggles which I had experienced while seeking to be baptized in the Holy Ghost. I warned them against allowing the devil to take advantage of their sincerity, making it difficult for their intellectual mind to release the control of their speech in order to allow the Holy Spirit to speak through them.

They fully committed their fears and reservations to Christ, and their mind was not concentrating on their speaking, or vocalization. Rather, their spirit was in tune with the Holy Spirit as he elevated their praises -- in their own language -- to a glorious, flowing river of worship ... lavishing praises upon the Father and his Son. The transition to praises in other tongues was spontaneous, taking no self-effort at all. When verbal syllables came out of their mouth which was not part of the word they were saying, they simply accepted it as a manifestation of the Holy Spirit which they had learned to accept as already dwelling within them.

They knew for themselves, without any doubt, that they had spoken as the Spirit had given them utterance. Some soon became quiet ... others were exuberant ... some praised and rejoiced for a long while ... others fell into pensive thought while basking in the presence of God -- and in fellowship of such loving saints -- because the entire church seemed to be re-baptized along with them. Joyous worship and praise flowed late into the night ... but no one cared about the late hour ... they were caught up in praise and worship.

What about the last Lady?

But, the lady who had been "tarrying" for twenty-five years was still seeking. I asked God if there was anything I could say to help her. I asked her a few questions, as I felt lead of the Lord. Her spirit seemed so dry, and her level of faith was at the bottom. She was aware that all the others were rejoicing in victory, and she alone was unfulfilled.

I asked her if, during the past twenty-five years, she had ever experienced any spontaneous praise, and was filled with joy and worship that seemed to flow out of her like an artesian well. I gave here the words of Christ:

- *JOH 7:38 He that believeth on me, as the scripture hath said, out of his belly shall flow rivers of living water.*
  39 (But this spake he of the Spirit, which they that believe on him should receive:

She said this had happened before, but not in a long time. It was obvious that disappointment had overpowered her courage to even expect an answer. She could not muster up any hope or excitement that she might be filled.

About groaning in the Spirit

The congregation became quiet as they listened carefully to me, because they were aware of her situation. I began to quietly seek for a word of wisdom from God who soon spoke into my spirit these words: "Ask her if she has ever <u>groaned</u> or <u>agonized</u> in the Spirit." I did so, and she replied that years ago this had happened to her. I then was prompted to ask her how long it had been since tears of joy and praise had come forth. She wondered why she could no longer cry ... which she had previously done ... in a deep and spiritually satisfying way.

I explained to her that those tears and groans were expressions of the Holy Spirit which he had demonstrated as normal human emotions quickened by the Spirit, but she had not recognized it, and had held back through timidity. I explained that God had given her a spoonful, but she had not received it by faith because it was not a shovelful, or a bucketful ... as the farmer had said to me.

I encouraged her to submit to the Spirit, and if she ever again experienced groaning, crying, or even stammering lips, to accept it by faith, and to give the Holy Ghost credit for whatever he was giving ... and, most of all, to not let the devil talk her out of accepting the beginnings of more to come.

She confessed that every time something happened that might have been the beginning of a manifestation of the Spirit, the devil was right there cautioning her to "be careful that you do not get in the flesh ... make sure it is the Holy Ghost, and not you." I quoted to her the following scriptures:

- *ROM 8:26 Likewise the Spirit also helpeth our infirmities: for we know not what we should pray for as we ought: but the Spirit itself maketh intercession for us with groanings which cannot be uttered.*
- *ISA 28:11 For with stammering lips and another tongue will he speak to this people.*
  12 To whom he said, This is the rest wherewith ye may cause the weary to rest; and this is the refreshing....

I told her that sometimes these groanings and stammering lips often precede fluent speaking in other tongues, and these must be accepted as coming from the Holy Spirit, and not from her mind or will.

I explained that Paul had said to the church, the spirit of the Prophet is subject unto the prophet, and one can suppress speaking in tongues aloud in the church when there is no interpreter present. It is evident, that by the same token we can suppress, or limit the Holy Spirit's ability to speak through us -- as she must have been doing ... for other reasons.

I laid hands on her by faith, and eyes that had been dry for years began to swell with tears. I felt certain God was about to rain on her desert. I encouraged her to accept those tears as a manifestation of the indwelling presence of the Holy Ghost. I was beginning to realize how close to the truth I actually was when I assured her the Holy Ghost had come into her a long time ago, but she had not been able to allow him to manifest his presence because she was trying to make sure it was not her doing the manifesting. You see, Satan was whispering in her ear, cautioning her to make sure it was the Holy Spirit speaking … and not her. Satan had been taking advantage of her honesty and sincerity.

To this she agreed, and the weeping became more intense. Her introverted sobbing changed into uninhibited crying … face open and upward. Her sorrowful crying soon shifted to crying for joy, filled with words of praise and adoration. It was not long before passionate groanings blended with her glorious worship.

With encouragement to accept all that was happening as coming from the anointing of the Spirit, and believing that the groanings by the Spirit were as authentic as speaking in other tongues, and just as scriptural, Syllables and phrases other than English began to intermingle with her words of praise, and she knew the utterances were coming forth by the Holy Ghost.

Very shortly thereafter she was speaking fluently in some foreign language, while the whole church exploded in praises, shouts of joy, worship, and adoration for Jesus the Baptizer, for the Holy Ghost, and for God the Father.

All chronic seekers had been gloriously baptized in the Holy Ghost.

Hallelujah!!

Allowing the Holy Spirit to speak in Tongues

I am sure there are many reading this book who are interested in experiencing God's gift of tongues. The first requirement according to God's word is that one must be a born again believer. God requires **confession** of sin, and **repentance** for those sins.

God also requires **believing the gospel** concerning him and his Son, Jesus Christ. God's first response to those who meet these requirements is to give them forgiveness, and to write their names in the Lamb's Book of Life, **and to authorize the Holy Ghost to abide within them.**

- *JOH 14:16 And I will pray the Father, and he shall give you another Comforter, that he may **abide** with you for ever; 17 Even the Spirit of truth; whom the world cannot receive, because it seeth him not, neither knoweth him: but ye know him; **for he dwelleth with you, and shall be in you.***

According to the word of God, they become new creatures in Christ Jesus, because they have been "**born again.**"

- *JOH 3:3 Jesus answered and said unto him, Verily, verily, I say unto thee, Except a man be born again, he cannot see the kingdom of God.*

- *ACT 2:38 Then Peter said unto them, Repent, and be baptized every one of you in the name of Jesus Christ for the remission of sins, and ye shall receive the gift of the Holy Ghost.*

- *1JO 1:9 If we **confess** our sins, he is faithful and just to forgive us our sins, and to cleanse us from all unrighteousness.*

- *MAR 1:15 And saying, The time is fulfilled, and the kingdom of God is at hand: **repent** ye, and **believe** the gospel.*

The gospel also contains truth regarding the Holy Spirit which must be believed.

Throughout the world there are millions of people who have been saved by God's grace, but due to a lack of correct preaching, or through erroneous teaching have never heard or understood the gospel truth concerning the baptism in the Holy Ghost.

Today, thankfully many have now heard this truth, and are aware that when they were saved God gave them the indwelling gift of the Holy Spirit. A great awakening concerning the Holy Spirit is occurring throughout the world, and the greatest area of growth among Christian believers involves millions who are embracing Biblical truth concerning the Baptism with the Holy Spirit, including speaking in other tongues as the Spirit gives the utterance.

Google News on the internet contains detailed information regarding this Holy Spirit conversion which is currently gaining much religious attention.

Presently, masses are hungering for the manifestation of speaking in other tongues as the Spirit gives them utterance.

- *ACT 2:4 And they were all filled with the Holy Ghost, and began to speak with other tongues, **as the Spirit gave them utterance.***

I encourage everyone seeking for the manifestation of speaking in other tongues to consciously pray to God in their normal language, while desiring, and remembering Biblically that when the Holy Spirit is praying in other tongues he is **speaking to God.**

- *1CO 14:2 For he that speaketh in an unknown tongue speaketh not unto men, **but unto God**: for no man understandeth him; howbeit in the spirit he speaketh mysteries.*

At this point one must submit to God in absolute faith, trusting and believing in his word. This gives a profound reason that one should believe the word of God regarding speaking in tongues.

That profound reason is that when the Holy Spirit is speaking in tongues, He is **speaking directly to God.**

When the Holy Ghost was praying in other tongues on the day of Pentecost, He was worshiping and praising God,

- *ACT 2:11 ... we do hear them speak in our tongues the wonderful works of God,*

Another aspect of speaking in tongues is that the Holy Spirit may be making **intercession** with God concerning the needs of the person through whom he is praying.

- *ROM 8:26 Likewise the Spirit also helpeth our infirmities: for we know not what we should pray for as we ought: but the Spirit itself maketh **intercession** for us with groanings which cannot be uttered* (which we could not utter).

One should not seek for speaking in tongues, but should concentrate on worship and praises to God, while believing in God as the giver of spiritual gifts.

During such prayer and worship, if unexpected syllables or words or utterances are injected among words you are praying, do not resist or attempt to correct it. Firmly believe that the Holy Spirit is blending his praises to God with your prayers, giving you utterances other than your own.

Support the utterances of the Spirit joyously and worshipfully, while waiting on the Lord.

- *ISA 40:31 But they that wait upon the LORD shall renew their strength; they shall mount up with wings as eagles; they shall run, and not be weary; and they shall walk, and not faint.*

You can pray alone, or it may be helpful to pray along with others who are supportive of your faith initiative.

Speaking in other tongues is just the beginning of a glorious and supernatural spiritual life through the indwelling of the Holy Ghost.

Much is contained in the Holy Scripture regarding the Holy Spirit, and such information should be carefully studied and believed. There are many Scriptural reasons why all who believe in Christ should allow the Holy Spirit to pray to God through them in other tongues. The first paramount reason is that this truth comes from the mouth of God through the Holy Scriptures. Whatever God says must be believed … and practiced!

- *MAT 4:4 But he answered and said, It is written, Man shall not live by bread alone, but by **every word that proceeded out of the mouth of God**.*

When God speaks concerning the Holy Spirit in his Holy Scriptures, one must pay close attention. It is easy for the carnal mind to disregard the importance of the Baptism in the Holy Ghost, which is important to God.

- *MAT 28:19 Go ye therefore, and teach all nations, **baptizing them in the name of the Father, and of the Son, <u>and of the Holy Ghost:</u>***
  20 <u>Teaching them</u> to observe all things whatsoever I have commanded you: and, lo, I am with you alway, even unto the end of the world.

Miraculous Confirmation

I will close this book with an experience which convinced me beyond any doubt that speaking in tongues can be a supernatural miracle that enables an ordinary person to speak in a language that is totally foreign to them.

I was in a home prayer meeting with fellow Christians, and as we prayed some began praying in other tongues. To everybody's surprise a lady who was speaking in tongues began making fairly loud clicking sounds with her tongue. As eyes began fastening on her, and all others looked at each other in perplexed wonder, the lady kept on clicking, and her expression appeared that she was totally bewildered, even more than we.

She kept on clicking for several minutes, and finally she returned to speaking in tongues, and joint worship continued. Naturally, everyone was wondering why such an event had occurred, and the lady could not understand what caused her to do such a thing.

She was totally bewildered as she explained how she was speaking in tongues, and she sensed a special anointing of the Holy Ghost came over her, and much to her surprise she began to make the clicking sounds which consisted of a variety of different types of clicks. She allowed it to continue because it seemed to her like the same spiritual force that prompted her to speak in tongues was also producing the clicking sounds.

After the meeting closed and I was on my way home, I talked to God concerning my bewilderment, and I believe God spoke to me to do an internet computer search to see if there existed a human language anywhere in the world that consisted of clicking sounds made with the tongue and mouth. I knew according to the Bible speaking in tongues consisted of a valid foreign language.

Of course, the first thing I did was get on the computer, and to my surprise, when I entered the search words, "clicking language," there popped onto the screen several documents containing information regarding a remote tribe in South Africa which speaks fluently by clicking sounds which played a major role in their communications which dated back through extinct tribes.

In my research I discovered that there exists in Africa certain tribes where their spoken language consists of a wide variety of clicking sounds. Most Click Speakers reside in Southeast Africa. Two major tribes are named the Hadzabe and the Sandawe, and are located near Lake Evasi, in Tanzania. Another Click Speaker tribe is named the Jul'hoansi.

Click speaking accurately describes what the woman was doing in the home prayer meeting. The common identification The terms "Click speakers" and "Click speaking" was used on the Internet in numerous articles by different authors.

Before writing this information today, I just did an updated Google computer search, and to my surprise there now exists extremely more information on the internet regarding a valid clicking language than when I first looked several years ago.

There can be no doubt that the Holy Spirit knew about this obscure remote language, and he chose to use it in giving utterance to the lady in the prayer meeting.

Regarding speaking in other tongues, the apostle Paul used the word "voices," and he said all voices (languages) have meaning somewhere in the world.

- *1CO 14:10 There are, it may be, so many kinds of voices in the world, and none of them is without signification.*

This means when one is speaking in other tongues, they are speaking in a language that is foreign to them, but they are speaking in a language which has a significant meaning somewhere in the world.

As I stand today, I could never have doubts about the supernatural, miraculous, authenticity of speaking in other tongues in a valid foreign language as the Holy Spirit gives the utterance of praise to God, as well as making intercession with God concerning the needs of the person praying.

I encourage everyone who is able to do so to make a computer search regarding "clicking language" ... followed by kneeling before God as a believer in his Holy Word. It is all in your Bible.

Anyone who is reading this book who has never spoken in tongues, listen carefully. If you know you are saved by God's grace, and have been born again as a child of God, and believe by faith that the gift of the Holy Ghost was given to you when you were born of the Spirit, but have never experienced the gift of speaking in other tongues, be assured ... you can enjoy that scriptural manifestation of the indwelling of the Holy Spirit ... according to the word of God.

The Bible says that when one speaks in tongues they are not speaking to men, but are speaking to God.

- *1CO 14:2 For he that speaketh in an unknown tongue speaketh not unto men, **but unto God**: for no man understandeth him; howbeit in the spirit he speaketh mysteries.*

The Bible says that when the Holy Spirit speaks to God he is either praising God, or he is making intercession for us concerning our needs.

- *ROM 8:26 Likewise the Spirit also helpeth our infirmities: for we know not what we should pray for as we ought: but the*

Spirit itself maketh intercession for us with groanings which cannot be uttered (meaning, which we could not utter).

There is no logical reason why anyone who believes in God would deprive themselves of sharing this blessed gift from God the Father.

I suggest that you frequently offer praises to God for truth in his word, and as you worship allow the Holy Spirit to inject utterances of syllables that are not from your words. Relax and allow the Holy Spirit to speak through you in praises to God, just as occurred on the day of Pentecost. It is all in the Bible!!! The Holy Ghost is able to speak audibly and distinctly in tongues other than ones native language. <u>The Holy Spirit gives the **utterance**</u>. Just believe the Bible by faith! Allow Him to speak even right now!!!

- *ACT 2:4 And they were all filled with the Holy Ghost, and began to speak with other tongues, <u>as the Spirit gave them utterance</u>.*
  5 And there were dwelling at Jerusalem Jews, devout men, out of every nation under heaven.
  6 Now when this was noised abroad, the multitude came together, and were confounded, because that every man heard them speak in his own language.
  7 And they were all amazed and marveled, saying one to another, Behold, are not all these which speak Galileans?
  8 And how hear we every man in our own tongue, wherein we were born ... we do hear them speak in our tongues the wonderful works of God.

God bless you as you go in the Spirit!

SPECIAL NOTICE: IF YOU HAVE BEEN BLESSED OR HELPED BY READING THIS BOOK, WE WOULD APPRECIATE HEARING FROM YOU. IF YOU ARE SPIRITUALLY HUNGRY TO OBTAIN A CLOSER WALK WITH GOD IN WAYS DESCRIBED IN THIS BOOK, PLEASE WRITE SO WE CAN PRAY WITH YOU, AND CALL YOUR NAME IN PRAYER BEFORE GOD. PLEASE WRITE.

SIGNED, Mac Ward Symes, Author

ADRESS CORRESPONDENCE TO:

ABOUT THE HOLY SPIRIT
P.O. BOX 7243
TYLER, TEXAS 75711.

GIVE YOUR NAME, PHONE NUMBER, ADDRESS, AND EMAIL -- AND YOU WILL BE WARMLY CONTACTED IN CHRISTIAN FELLOWSHIP.

This Book is Written by Mac Ward Symes
A Minister of Christ

1CO 4:1 Let a man so account of us, as of the <u>ministers of Christ</u>, and stewards of the mysteries of God.

Mac Ward Symes and wife, Margaret Elizabeth Symes work together as a ministerial team.

We would appreciate receiving a letter giving your written testimony regarding God's gift of Grace.

"Please give your contact information so that we may respond, Include Name, Address, Telephone Number, Email"

Contact Information:
Mac & Margaret Symes
P.O. Box 7243
Tyler, Texas 75711

<u>Regarding Phone or Mail Orders for this Book:</u>

BOOK TITLE: "<u>ABOUT THE HOLY SPIRIT</u>"

Pay By
**VISA – MasterCARD – DISCOVER –
AMERICAN EXPRESS**
Personal Check
Call – 903-520-0522

ORDER BOOK FROM AUTHOR
MAC WARD SYMES
P.O. BOX 7243
TYLER, TX 75711
903-520-0522

<u>**ORDER BOOK FROM PUBLISHER**</u>
WESTBOW PRESS
1663 LIBERTY DRIVE
BLOOMINGTON, IN 47403
PHONE: 866-928-1240

PURCHASE OR ORDER FROM MAJOR BOOK SELLERS

MAJOR BOOK STORES:
AMAZON BOOKS -- BARNES & NOBLE --
POWELL'S BOOKS -- THE HUDSON GROUP --
BOOKS-A-MILLION – BOOKS INC. – COKESBURY

ANY STORE THAT DOES NOT HAVE THE BOOK,
"ABOUT THE HOLY SPIRIT," IN STOCK, WILL
USUALLY ORDER FOR YOU AT NO EXTRA CHARGE.

Necessary Information:
On Mail Orders
Print Name and Address
Check or Credit Card info

On Phone Orders
Give Name, Check or Credit Card information,
Shipping Address, Driver's License Info

The author, **Mac Ward Symes**, wrote another book entitled

"SHOULD ALL SPEAK WITH TONGUES"

which is an amazing sequel to this book entitled
"ABOUT THE HOLY SPIRIT,"
and should be read by every person desiring more
Biblical information regarding The Holy Spirit.

You may order the book from

WestBow Press
(844) 714-3454
Amazon
(888) 280-4331
Barnes & Noble
(800) 843-2665

Or order from your favorite bookstore.

If a bookstore does not have the book in stock, they can order it
for you by the book name.

The two books written by author, **Mac Ward
Symes**, and published by **WestBow Press:**
1663 Liberty Drive
Bloomington, IN 47403

"SHOULD ALL SPEAK WITH TONGUES"

"ABOUT THE HOLY SPIRIT"

Printed in the United States
by Baker & Taylor Publisher Services

Printed in the United States
by Baker & Taylor Publisher Services